The JESUS BOOK

Everything The Father Wanted You To Know About His Son

MIKE MURDOCK

Unless otherwise indicated, all Scripture quotations are taken from the *King James Version* of the Bible.

The Jesus Book
Copyright © 1990 by Mike Murdock
ISBN 156394-002-7

Published by Wisdom International
P. O. Box 99
Denton, Texas 76202

TABLE OF CONTENTS

TOPIC   **PAGE**

∼ 1 ∼

THE ACHIEVEMENTS OF JESUS

"And Jesus answering said unto him, Suffer it to be so now: for thus it becometh us to fulfil all righteousness. Then he suffered Him. And Jesus, when He was baptized, went up straightway out of the water: and, lo, the heavens were opened unto Him, and he saw the Spirit of God descending like a dove, and lighting upon Him: And lo a voice from heaven, saying, This is My beloved Son, in Whom I am well pleased" (Matthew 3:15-17).

"That it might be fulfilled which was spoken by Esaias the prophet, saying, The land of Zabulon, and the land of Nephthalim, by the way of the sea, beyond Jordan, Galilee of the Gentiles; The people which sat in darkness saw great light; and to them which sat in the region and shadow of death light is sprung up. From that time Jesus began to preach, and to say, Repent: for the kingdom of heaven is at hand" (Matthew 4:14-17).

"Think not that I am come to destroy the law, or the prophets: I am not come to destroy, but to fulfil" (Matthew 5:17).

"That it might be fulfilled which was spoken by Esaias the prophet, saying, Himself took our infirmities, and bare our sicknesses" (Matthew 8:17).

"And it came to pass, when Jesus had finished all these sayings, He said unto His disciples, Ye know that after two days is the feast of the passover, and the Son of man is betrayed to be crucified" (Matthew 26:1,2).

"The Spirit of the Lord is upon Me, because He hath anointed Me to preach the gospel to the poor; He hath sent Me to heal the brokenhearted, to preach deliverance to the captives, and recovering of sight to the blind, to set at liberty them that are bruised, To preach the acceptable year of the Lord. And He closed the book, and He gave it again to the minister, and sat down. And the eyes of all them that were in the synagogue were fastened on Him. And He began to say unto them, This day is this Scripture fulfilled in your ears" (Luke 4:18-21).

"Then He took unto Him the twelve, and said unto them, Behold, we go up to Jerusalem, and all things that are written by the prophets concerning the Son of man shall be accomplished" (Luke 18:31).

"For the Son of man is come to seek and to save that which was lost" (Luke 19:10).

"For I say unto you, that this that is written must yet be accomplished in Me, And He was reckoned among the transgressors: for the things concerning Me have an end" (Luke 22:37).

"And He said unto them, These are the words which I spake unto you, while I was yet with you, that all things must be fulfilled, which were written in the law of Moses, and in the prophets, and in the psalms, concerning Me" (Luke 24:44).

"For I came down from heaven, not to do mine own will, but the will of Him that sent Me. And this is the Father's will which hath sent Me, that of all which He hath given Me I should lose nothing, but should raise it up again at the last day" (John 6:38,39).

"And there are also many other things which Jesus did, the which, if they should be written every one, I suppose that even the world itself could not contain the books that should be written. Amen" (John 21:25).

"Wherefore He is able also to save them to the uttermost that come unto God by Him, seeing He ever liveth to make intercession for them" (Hebrews 7:25).

"Then said I, Lo, I come (in the volume of the book it is written of Me, to do Thy will,) O God" (Hebrews 10:7).

"And the Holy Ghost descended in a bodily shape like a dove upon Him, and a voice came from heaven, which said, Thou art My beloved Son; in Thee I am well pleased." (Luke 3:22)

~ 2 ~

THE ANOINTING
OF JESUS

"And Jesus, immediately knowing in Himself that virtue had gone out of Him, turned Him about in the press, and said, Who touched My clothes?" (Mark 5:30).

"And the angel answered and said unto her, The Holy Ghost shall come upon thee, and the power of the Highest shall overshadow thee: therefore also that holy thing which shall be born of thee shall be called the Son of God" (Luke 1:35).

"And the Holy Ghost descended in a bodily shape like a dove upon Him, and a voice came from heaven, which said, Thou art My beloved Son; in Thee I am well pleased" (Luke 3:22).

"And Jesus being full of the Holy Ghost returned from Jordan, and was led by the Spirit into the wilderness, And Jesus returned in the power of the Spirit into Galilee: and there went out a fame of Him through all the region round about. The Spirit of the Lord is upon Me, because He hath anointed Me to preach the gospel to the poor; He hath sent Me to heal the brokenhearted, to preach deliverance to the captives, and recovering of sight to the blind, to set at liberty them that are bruised, To preach the acceptable year of the Lord. And they were all amazed, and spake among themselves, saying, What a word is this! for with authority and power He commandeth the unclean spirits, and they come out" (Luke 4:1,14,18,19,36).

"And the whole multitude sought to touch Him: for there went virtue out of Him, and healed them all" (Luke 6:19).

"And Jesus said, Somebody hath touched Me: for I perceive that virtue is gone out of Me. And when the woman saw that she was not hid, she came trembling, and falling down before Him, she declared unto Him before all the people for what cause she had touched Him, and how she was healed immediately" (Luke 8:46,47).

"And John bare record, saying, I saw the Spirit descending from heaven like a dove, and it abode upon Him. And I knew Him not: but He that sent me to baptize with water, the same said unto me, Upon whom thou shalt see the Spirit descending, and remaining on Him, the same is He which baptizeth with the Holy Ghost" (John 1:32,33).

"For He whom God hath sent speaketh the words of God: for God giveth not the Spirit by measure unto Him. The Father loveth the Son, and hath given all things into His hand. He that believeth on the Son hath everlasting life: and he that believeth not the Son shall not see life; but the wrath of God abideth on him" (John 3:34-36).

"For of a truth against thy holy child Jesus, Whom Thou hast anointed, both Herod, and Pontius Pilate, with the Gentiles, and the people of Israel, were gathered together" (Acts 4:27).

"How God anointed Jesus of Nazareth with the Holy Ghost and with power: Who went about doing good, and healing all that were oppressed of the devil; for God was with Him" (Acts 10:38).

≈ 3 ≈

THE APPEARANCE OF JESUS

⟨━━━⊃●⊂━━━⟩

"As many were astonied at thee; His visage was so marred more than any man, and His form more than the sons of men" (Isaiah 52:14).

"For He shall grow up before Him as a tender plant, and as a root out of a dry ground: He hath no form nor comeliness; and when we shall see Him, there is no beauty that we should desire Him. He is despised and rejected of men; a man of sorrows, and acquainted with grief: and we hid as it were our faces from Him; He was despised, and we esteemed Him not. Surely He hath borne our griefs, and carried our sorrows: yet we did esteem Him stricken, smitten of God, and afflicted. But He was wounded for our transgressions, He was bruised for our iniquities: the chastisement of our peace was upon Him; and with His stripes we are healed" (Isaiah 53:2-5).

"And after six days Jesus taketh with Him Peter, and James, and John, and leadeth them up into an high mountain apart by themselves: and He was transfigured before them. And His raiment became shining, exceeding white as snow; so as no fuller on earth can white them" (Mark 9:2,3).

"And Jesus said, I am: and ye shall see the Son

of man sitting on the right hand of power, and coming in the clouds of heaven" (Mark 14:62).

"And Jesus increased in wisdom and stature, and in favour with God and man" (Luke 2:52).

"And as He prayed, the fashion of His countenance was altered, and His raiment was white and glistering" (Luke 9:29).

"Then came Jesus forth, wearing the crown of thorns, and the purple robe. And Pilate saith unto them, Behold the man!" (John 19:5).

"And said, Behold, I see the heavens opened, and the Son of man standing on the right hand of God" (Acts 7:56).

"But made Himself of no reputation, and took upon Him the form of a servant, and was made in the likeness of men: And being found in fashion as a man, He humbled Himself, and became obedient unto death, even the death of the cross" (Philippians 2:7,8).

"Who being the brightness of His glory, and the express image of His person, and upholding all things by the word of His power, when He had by Himself purged our sins, sat down on the right hand of the Majesty on high" (Hebrews 1:3).

"And in the midst of the seven candlesticks one like unto the Son of man, clothed with a garment down to the foot, and girt about the paps with a golden girdle. His head and His hairs were white like wool, as white as snow; and His eyes were as a flame of fire; And His feet like unto fine brass, as if they burned in a furnace; and His voice as the sound of many waters. And He had in His right hand seven stars: and out of His mouth went a sharp twoedged sword: and His countenance was as the sun shineth in His strength" (Revelation 1:13-16).

"And I looked, and behold a white cloud, and upon the cloud one sat like unto the Son of man, having on His head a golden crown, and in His hand a sharp sickle" (Revelation 14:14).

"His eyes were as a flame of fire, and on His head were many crowns; and He had a name written, that no man knew, but He Himself. And He was clothed with a vesture dipped in blood: and His name is called The Word of God. And out of His mouth goeth a sharp sword, that with it He should smite the nations: and He shall rule them with a rod of iron: and He treadeth the winepress of the fierceness and wrath of Almighty God. And He hath on His vesture and on His thigh a name written, King of Kings, And Lord Of Lords" (Revelation 19:12,13,15, 16).

"And He took a child, and set him in the midst of them: and when He had taken him in His arms, He said unto them, Whosoever shall receive one of such children in My name, receiveth Me: and whosoever shall receive Me, receiveth not Me, but Him that sent Me." (Mark 9:36,37)

⁓ 4 ⁓

THE ATTITUDE OF JESUS

"Therefore I say unto you, Take no thought for your life, what ye shall eat, or what ye shall drink; nor yet for your body, what ye shall put on. Is not the life more than meat, and the body than raiment? Take therefore no thought for the morrow: for the morrow shall take thought for the things of itself. Sufficient unto the day is the evil thereof" (Matthew 6:25,34).

"And He took a child, and set him in the midst of them: and when He had taken him in His arms, He said unto them, Whosoever shall receive one of such children in My name, receiveth Me: and whosoever shall receive Me, receiveth not Me, but Him that sent Me" (Mark 9:36,37).

"The Spirit of the Lord is upon Me, because He hath anointed Me to preach the gospel to the poor; He hath sent Me to heal the brokenhearted, to preach deliverance to the captives, and recovering of sight to the blind, to set at liberty them that are bruised, To preach the acceptable year of the Lord. And He closed the book, and He gave it again to the minister, and sat down. And the eyes of all them that were in the synagogue were fastened on Him. And He began to say unto them, This day is this Scripture fulfilled in your ears. And all bare Him witness, and wondered at the gracious words which proceeded out of His mouth. And they said, Is not this Joseph's son?" (Luke 4:18-22).

"But a certain Samaritan, as he journeyed, came where he was: and when he saw him, he had compassion on him, And went to him, and bound up his wounds, pouring in oil and wine, and set him on his own beast, and brought him to an inn, and took care of him. And on the morrow when he departed, he took out two pence, and gave them to the host, and said unto him, Take care of him; and whatsoever thou spendest more, when I come again, I will repay thee. Which now of these three, thinkest thou, was neighbor unto him that fell among the thieves? And he said, He that shewed mercy on him. Then said Jesus unto him, Go, and do thou likewise" (Luke 10:33-37).

"After that He poureth water into a bason, and began to wash the disciples' feet, and to wipe them with the towel wherewith He was girded. Then cometh He to Simon Peter: and Peter saith unto Him, Lord, dost thou wash my feet? Jesus answered and said unto him, What I do thou knowest not now; but thou shalt know hereafter. Peter saith unto Him, Thou shalt never wash my feet. Jesus answered him, If I wash thee not, thou hast no part with Me. Simon Peter saith unto Him, Lord, not my feet only, but also my hands and my head. Jesus saith to him, He that is washed needeth not save to wash his feet, but is clean every whit: and ye are clean, but not all" (John 13:5-10).

"But made Himself of no reputation, and took upon Him the form of a servant, and was made in the likeness of men: And being found in fashion as a man, He humbled Himself, and became obedient unto death, even the death of the cross" (Philippians 2:7,8).

～ 5 ～

THE AUTHORITY OF JESUS

"But that ye may know that the Son of man hath power on earth to forgive sins, (then saith He to the sick of the palsy,) Arise, take up thy bed, and go unto thine house. And he arose, and departed to his house. But when the multitude saw it, they marvelled, and glorified God, which had given such power unto men" (Matthew 9:6-8).

"And when He had called unto Him His twelve disciples, He gave them power against unclean spirits, to cast them out, and to heal all manner of sickness and all manner of disease" (Matthew 10:1).

"And when He was come into the temple, the chief priests and the elders of the people came unto Him as He was teaching, and said, By what authority doest Thou these things? and who gave Thee this authority? And Jesus answered and said unto them, I also will ask you one thing, which if ye tell Me, I in like wise will tell you by what authority I do these things. The baptism of John, whence was it? from heaven, or of men? And they reasoned with themselves, saying, If we shall say, From heaven; He will say unto us, Why did ye not then believe Him? But if we shall say, Of men; we fear the people; for all hold John as a prophet. And they answered Jesus, and said, We cannot tell. And He said unto them, Neither tell I you by what authority I do these things" (Matthew 21:23-27).

"And Jesus came and spake unto them, saying, All power is given unto Me in heaven and in earth" (Matthew 28:18).

"And they were astonished at His doctrine: for He taught them as one that had authority, and not as the scribes. And they were all amazed, insomuch that they questioned among themselves, saying, What thing is this? what new doctrine is this? for with authority commandeth He even the unclean spirits, and they do obey Him" (Mark 1:22,27).

"And He called unto Him the twelve, and began to send them forth by two and two; and gave them power over unclean spirits" (Mark 6:7).

"And they were astonished at His doctrine: for His word was with power. And they were all amazed, and spake among themselves, saying, What a word is this! for with authority and power He commandeth the uncleaned spirits, and they come out" (Luke 4:32,36).

"But that ye may know that the Son of man hath power upon earth to forgive sins, (He said unto the sick of the palsy,) I say unto thee, Arise, and take up thy couch, and go into thine house" (Luke 5:24).

"Behold, I give unto you power to tread on serpents and scorpions, and over all the power of the enemy: and nothing shall by any means hurt you" (Luke 10:19).

"To the only wise God our Saviour, be glory and majesty, dominion and power, both now and for ever. Amen" (Jude 1:25).

"The Revelation of Jesus Christ, which God gave unto Him, to shew unto His servants things which must shortly come to pass; and He sent and signified it by His angel unto His servant John" (Revelation 1:1).

～ 6 ～

THE BAPTISM OF JESUS

"I indeed baptize you with water unto repentance: but He that cometh after me is mightier than I, whose shoes I am not worthy to bear: He shall baptize you with the Holy Ghost, and with fire: And Jesus answering said unto him, Suffer it to be so now: for thus it becometh us to fulfil all righteousness. Then he suffered Him. And Jesus, when He was baptized, went up straightway out of the water: and, lo, the heavens were opened unto Him, and he saw the Spirit of God descending like a dove, and lighting upon Him" (Matthew 3:11,15,16).

"I indeed have baptized you with water: but He shall baptize you with the Holy Ghost. And it came to pass in those days, that Jesus came from Nazareth of Galilee, and was baptized of John in Jordan. And straightway coming up out of the water, he saw the heavens opened, and the Spirit like a dove descending upon Him" (Mark 1:8-10).

"John answered, saying unto them all, I indeed baptize you with water; but one mightier than I cometh, the latchet of whose shoes I am not worthy to unloose: He shall baptize you with the Holy Ghost and with fire: Now when all the people were baptized, it came to pass, that Jesus also being baptized, and praying, the heaven was opened, And the Holy Ghost descended in a bodily shape like a dove upon Him, and a voice came from heaven, which said, Thou art My beloved Son; in thee I am well pleased" (Luke 3:16,21,22).

"The next day John seeth Jesus coming unto him, and saith, Behold the Lamb of God, which taketh away the sin of the world. This is He of whom I said, After me cometh a man which is preferred before me: for He was before me. And I knew Him not: but that He should be made manifest to Israel, therefore am I come baptizing with water. And John bare record, saying, I saw the Spirit descending from heaven like a dove, and it abode upon Him. And I knew Him not: but He that sent me to baptize with water, the same said unto me, Upon Whom thou shalt see the Spirit descending, and remaining on Him, the same is He which baptizeth with the Holy Ghost. And I saw, and bare record that this is the Son of God" (John 1:29-34).

"Then said Paul, John verily baptized with the baptism of repentance, saying unto the people, that they should believe on Him which should come after him, that is, on Christ Jesus. When they heard this, they were baptized in the name of the Lord Jesus" (Acts 19:4,5).

"Know ye not, that so many of us as were baptized into Jesus Christ were baptized into His death?" (Romans 6:3).

"For as many of you as have been baptized into Christ have put on Christ" (Galatians 3:27).

≈ 7 ≈

THE BEATITUDES OF JESUS

"And seeing the multitudes, He went up into a mountain: and when He was set, His disciples came unto Him: And He opened His mouth, and taught them, saying, Blessed are the poor in spirit: for their's is the kingdom of heaven. Blessed are they that mourn: for they shall be comforted. Blessed are the meek: for they shall inherit the earth. Blessed are they which do hunger and thirst after righteousness: for they shall be filled. Blessed are the merciful: for they shall obtain mercy. Blessed are the pure in heart: for they shall see God. Blessed are the peacemakers: for they shall be called the children of God. Blessed are they which are persecuted for righteousness' sake: for their's is the kingdom of heaven. Blessed are ye, when men shall revile you, and persecute you, and shall say all manner of evil against you falsely, for My sake. Rejoice, and be exceeding glad: for great is your reward in heaven: for so persecuted they the prophets which were before you. Ye are the salt of the earth: but if the salt have lost his savour, wherewith shall it be salted? it is thenceforth good for nothing, but to be cast out, and to be trodden under foot of men" (Matthew 5:1-13).

"In the beginning was the Word, and the Word was with God, and the Word was God."   (John 1:1)

≈ 8 ≈

THE BEGINNING OF JESUS

"In the beginning was the Word, and the Word was with God, and the Word was God" (John 1:1).

"The same was in the beginning with God" (John 1:2).

"John bare witness of Him and cried, saying, This was He of whom I spake, He that cometh after me is preferred before me: for He was before me. This is He of whom I said, After me cometh a man which is preferred before me: for He was before me" (John 1:15,30).

"And He said unto them, Ye are from beneath; I am from above: ye are of this world; I am not of this world. Jesus said unto them, Verily, verily, I say unto you, Before Abraham was, I am" (John 8:23,58).

"Believest thou not that I am in the Father, and the Father in Me? the words that I speak unto you I speak not of Myself: but the Father that dwelleth in Me, He doeth the works" (John 14:10).

"Pilate therefore said unto Him, Art thou a king then? Jesus answered, Thou sayest that I am a king. To this end was I born, and for this cause came I into the world, that I should bear witness unto the truth. Every one that is of the truth heareth My voice" (John 18:37).

"And to make all men see what is the fellowship of the mystery, which from the beginning of the world hath been hid in God, who created all things by Jesus

Christ" (Ephesians 3:9).

"Who is the image of the invisible God, the firstborn of every creature: For by Him were all things created, that are in heaven, and that are in earth, visible and invisible, whether they be thrones, or dominions, or principalities, or powers: all things were created by Him, and for Him: And He is before all things, and by Him all things consist. And He is the head of the body, the church: who is the beginning, the firstborn from the dead; that in all things He might have the preeminence" (Colossians 1:15-18).

"Hath in these last days spoken unto us by His Son, Whom He hath appointed heir of all things, by Whom also He made the worlds; And again, when He bringeth in the first begotten into the world, He saith, And let all the angels of God worship Him. But unto the Son He saith, Thy throne, O God, is for ever and ever: a sceptre of righteousness is the sceptre of Thy kingdom" (Hebrews 1:2,6,8).

"Without father, without mother, without descent, having neither beginning of days, nor end of life; but made like unto the Son of God; abideth a priest continually" (Hebrews 7:3).

"And when I saw Him, I fell at His feet as dead. And He laid His right hand upon me, saying unto me, Fear not; I am the first and the last" (Revelation 1:17).

"And He said unto me, It is done. I am Alpha and Omega, the beginning and the end. I will give unto him that is athirst of the fountain of the water of life freely" (Revelation 21:6).

❧ 9 ❧

THE BETRAYAL OF JESUS

"Simon the Canaanite, and Judas Iscariot, who also betrayed him" (Matthew 10:4).

"And while they abode in Galilee, Jesus said unto them, The Son of man shall be betrayed into the hands of men" (Matthew 17:22).

"Behold we go up to Jerusalem; and the Son of man shall be betrayed unto the chief priests and unto the scribes, and they shall condemn Him to death" (Matthew 20:18).

"Ye know that after two days is the feast of the passover, and the Son of man is betrayed to be crucified. And from that time he sought opportunity to betray Him. And as they did eat, He said, Verily I say unto you, that one of you shall betray Me. And He answered and said, He that dippeth his hand with Me in the dish, the same shall betray Me. The Son of man goeth as it is written of Him: but woe unto that man by whom the Son of man is betrayed! it had been good for that man if he had not been born. Then Judas, which betrayed Him, answered and said, Master, is it I? He said unto him, Thou hast said. Then cometh He to His disciples, and saith unto them, Sleep on now, and take your rest: behold, the hour is at hand, and the Son of man is betrayed into the hands of sinners. Rise, let us be going: behold, he is at hand that doth betray Me. Now he that betrayed Him gave them a sign, saying, Whomsoever I shall kiss, that same is He: hold Him fast" (Matthew 26:2,16,21,23-25,45,46,48).

"Then Judas, which had betrayed Him, when he saw that He was condemned, repented himself, and brought again the thirty pieces of silver to the chief priests and elders, Saying, I have sinned in that I have betrayed the innocent blood. And they said, What is that to us? see thou to that" (Matthew 27:3,4).

"But there are some of you that believe not. For Jesus knew from the beginning who they were that believed not, and who should betray Him" (John 6:64).

"And Judas also, which betrayed Him, knew the place: for Jesus ofttimes resorted thither with His disciples" (John 18:2).

"Then Peter, turning about, seeth the disciple whom Jesus loved following; which also leaned on his breast at supper, and said, Lord, which is he that betrayeth Thee?" (John 21:20).

"Which of the prophets have not your fathers persecuted? and they have slain them which shewed before of the coming of the Just One; of whom ye have been now the betrayers and murderers" (Acts 7:52).

"For I have received of the Lord that which also I delivered unto you, That the Lord Jesus the same night in which he was betrayed took bread" (1 Corinthians 11:23).

❦ 10 ❦

THE BIRTH OF JESUS

"Therefore the Lord Himself shall give you a sign; Behold, a virgin shall conceive, and bear a son, and shall call His name Immanuel" (Isaiah 7:14).

"But thou, Bethlehem Ephratah, though thou be little among the thousands of Judah, yet out of thee shall He come forth unto Me that is to be ruler in Israel; whose goings forth have been from of old, from everlasting" (Micah 5:2).

"Now the birth of Jesus Christ was on this wise: When as His mother Mary was espoused to Joseph, before they came together, she was found with child of the Holy Ghost. But while he thought on these things, behold, the angel of the Lord appeared unto him in a dream, saying, Joseph, thou son of David, fear not to take unto thee Mary thy wife: for that which is conceived in her is of the Holy Ghost" (Matthew 1:18,20).

"Now when Jesus was born in Bethlehem of Judaea in the days of Herod the king, behold, there came wise men from the east to Jerusalem, And he sent them to Bethlehem, and said, Go and search diligently for the young child; and when ye have found Him, bring me word again, that I may come and worship Him also. When they had heard the king, they departed; and, lo, the star, which they saw in the east, went before them, till it came and stood over where the young child was. When they saw the star, they rejoiced with exceeding great joy. And when they were come into the house, they saw the young child with Mary His mother, and fell down, and worshipped Him: and when they had opened their treasures, they presented unto Him gifts; gold, and frankincense, and myrrh" (Matthew 2:1,8-11).

"And thou shalt have joy and gladness; and many shall rejoice at His birth. And the angel answered and said unto her, The Holy Ghost shall come upon thee, and the power of the Highest shall overshadow thee: therefore also that holy thing which shall be born of thee shall be called the Son of God" (Luke 1:14,35).

"And she brought forth her firstborn son, and wrapped Him in swaddling clothes, and laid Him in a manger; because there was no room for them in the inn. And the angel said unto them, Fear not: for, behold, I bring you good tidings of great joy, which shall be to all people. For unto you is born this day in the city of David a Saviour, which is Christ the Lord. And this shall be a sign unto you; Ye shall find the babe wrapped in swaddling clothes, lying in a manger. And suddenly there was with the angel a multitude of the heavenly hosts praising God, and saying, Glory to God in the highest, and on earth peace, good will toward men. And they came with haste, and found Mary, and Joseph, and the babe lying in a manger" (Luke 2:7,10-14,16).

"Pilate therefore said unto Him, Art thou a king then? Jesus answered, Thou sayest that I am a king. To this end was I born, and for this cause came I into the world, that I should bear witness unto the truth. Every one that is of the truth heareth My voice" (John 18:37).

⁓ 11 ⁓

THE BLOOD OF JESUS

"For this is My blood of the new testament, which is shed for many for the remission of sins" (Matthew 26:28).

"And being in an agony He prayed more earnestly: and His sweat was as it were great drops of blood falling down to the ground" (Luke 22:44).

"Then Jesus said unto them, Verily, verily, I say unto you, Except ye eat the flesh of the Son of man, and drink His blood, ye have no life in you. Whoso eateth My flesh, and drinketh My blood, hath eternal life; and I will raise him up at the last day. For My flesh is meat indeed, and My blood is drink indeed" (John 6:53-55).

"But one of the soldiers with a spear pierced His side, and forthwith came there out blood and water" (John 19:34).

"Saying, Did not we straitly command you that ye should not teach in this name? and, behold, ye have filled Jerusalem with your doctrine, and intend to bring this man's blood upon us" (Acts 5:28).

"Take heed therefore unto yourselves, and to all the flock, over the which the Holy Ghost hath made you overseers, to feed the church of God, which He hath purchased with His own blood" (Acts 20:28).

"Whom God hath set forth to be a propitiation through faith in His blood, to declare His righteousness for the remission of sins that are past, through the forbearance of God" (Romans 3:25).

"The cup of blessing which we bless, is it not the communion of the blood of Christ? The bread which we break, is it not the communion of the body of Christ?" (1 Corinthians 10:16).

"Wherefore whosoever shall eat this bread, and drink this cup of the Lord, unworthily, shall be guilty of the body and blood of the Lord" (1 Corinthians 11:27).

"In Whom we have redemption through His blood, the forgiveness of sins, according to the riches of His grace" (Ephesians 1:7).

"Neither by the blood of goats and calves, but by His own blood He entered in once into the holy place, having obtained eternal redemption for us" (Hebrews 9:12).

"Having therefore, brethren, boldness to enter into the holiest by the blood of Jesus" (Hebrews 10:19).

"Wherefore Jesus also, that He might sanctify the people with His own blood, suffered without the gate" (Hebrews 13:12).

"But if we walk in the light, as He is in the light, we have fellowship one with another, and the blood of Jesus Christ His Son cleanseth us from all sin" (1 John 1:7).

"And from Jesus Christ, Who is the faithful witness, and the first begotten of the dead, and the prince of the kings of the earth. Unto Him that loved us, and washed us from our sins in His own blood" (Revelation 1:5).

"And they sung a new song, saying, Thou art

worthy to take the book, and to open the seals thereof: for Thou wast slain, and hast redeemed us to God by Thy blood out of every kindred, and tongue, and people, and nation" (Revelation 5:9).

"And I said unto Him, Sir, thou knowest. And He said to me, These are they which came out of great tribulation, and have washed their robes, and made them white in the blood of the Lamb" (Revelation 7:14).

"And they overcame him by the blood of the Lamb, and by the word of their testimony; and they loved not their lives unto the death" (Revelation 12:11).

"But when He saw the multitudes, He was moved with compassion on them, because they fainted, and were scattered abroad, as sheep having no shepherd."
(Matthew 9:36)

~ 12 ~

THE CHARACTER OF JESUS

"But when He saw the multitudes, He was moved with compassion on them, because they fainted, and were scattered abroad, as sheep having no shepherd" (Matthew 9:36).

"And Jesus went forth, and saw a great multitude, and was moved with compassion toward them, and He healed their sick" (Matthew 14:14).

"Then Jesus called His disciples unto Him, and said, I have compassion on the multitude, because they continue with Me now three days, and have nothing to eat: and I will not send them away fasting, lest they faint in the way" (Matthew 15:32).

"And Jesus, moved with compassion, put forth His hand, and touched him, and saith unto him, I will; be thou clean" (Mark 1:41).

"Howbeit Jesus suffered him not, but saith unto him, Go home to thy friends, and tell them how great things the Lord hath done for thee, and hath had compassion on thee" (Mark 5:19).

"And Jesus, when He came out, saw much people, and was moved with compassion toward them, because they were as sheep not having a shepherd: and He began to teach them many things" (Mark 6:34).

"And they brought young children to Him, that He should touch them: and His disciples rebuked those that brought them. But when Jesus saw it, He was much displeased, and said unto them, Suffer the little children to come unto Me, and forbid them not: for of such is the kingdom of God. Then Jesus beholding him loved him, and said unto him, One thing thou lackest: go thy way, sell whatsoever thou hast, and give to the poor, and thou shalt have treasure in heaven: and come, take up the cross, and follow Me" (Mark 10:13,14,21).

"But He held His peace, and answered nothing. Again the high priest asked Him, and said unto Him, Art thou the Christ, the Son of the Blessed?" (Mark 14:61).

"And the chief priests accused Him of many things: but He answered nothing" (Mark 15:3).

"O Jerusalem, Jerusalem, which killest the prophets, and stonest them that are sent unto thee; how often would I have gathered thy children together, as a hen doth gather her brood under her wings, and ye would not!" (Luke 13:34).

"But Jesus called them unto him, and said, Suffer little children to come unto Me, and forbid them not: for of such is the kingdom of God" (Luke 18:16).

"Now Jesus loved Martha, and her sister, and Lazarus" (John 11:5).

"Now before the feast of the passover, when Jesus knew that His hour was come that He should depart out of this world unto the Father, having loved His own which were in the world, He loved them unto the end" (John 13:1).

"He that hath My commandments, and keepeth them, he it is that loveth Me: and he that loveth Me shall be loved of My Father, and I will love him, and will manifest Myself to him" (John 14:21).

"Then said Jesus unto Peter, Put up thy sword into the sheath: the cup which My Father hath given Me, shall I not drink it?" (John 18:11).

"Pilate therefore went forth again, and saith unto them, Behold, I bring Him forth to you, that ye may know that I find no fault in Him" (John 19:4).

"But ye denied the Holy One and the Just, and desired a murderer to be granted unto you" (Acts 3:14).

"Husbands, love your wives, even as Christ also loved the church, and gave Himself for it" (Ephesians 5:25).

"The Lord is not slack concerning His promise, as some men count slackness; but is longsuffering to us-ward, not willing that any should perish, but that all should come to repentance" (2 Peter 3:9).

"If we confess our sins, He is faithful and just to forgive us our sins, and to cleanse us from all unrighteousness" (1 John 1:9).

"And from Jesus Christ, who is the faithful witness, and the first begotten of the dead, and the prince of the kings of the earth. Unto Him that loved us, and washed us from our sins in His own blood" (Revelation 1:5).

"As many as I love, I rebuke and chasten: be zealous therefore, and repent" (Revelation 3:19).

"And Jesus went about all Galilee, teaching in their synagogues, and preaching the gospel of the kingdom, and healing all manner of sickness and all manner of disease among the people."

(Matthew 4:23)

≈ 13 ≈

THE CHURCH ATTENDANCE OF JESUS

"And Jesus went about all Galilee, teaching in their synagogues, and preaching the gospel of the kingdom, and healing all manner of sickness and all manner of disease among the people" (Matthew 4:23).

"And Jesus went about all the cities and villages, teaching in their synagogues, and preaching the gospel of the kingdom, and healing every sickness and every disease among the people" (Matthew 9:35).

"And when He was departed thence, He went into their synagogue" (Matthew 12:9).

"And when He was come into His own country, He taught them in their synagogue, insomuch that they were astonished, and said, Whence hath this man this wisdom, and these mighty works?" (Matthew 13:54).

"For where two or three are gathered together in My name, there am I in the midst of them" (Matthew 18:20).

"And Jesus went into the temple of God, and cast out all them that sold and bought in the temple, and overthrew the tables of the moneychangers, and the seats of them that sold doves, And said unto them, It is written, My house shall be called the house of prayer; but ye have made it a den of thieves" (Matthew 21:12,13).

"And they went into Capernaum; and straightway on the sabbath day He entered into the synagogue, and taught" (Mark 1:21).

"And He entered again into the synagogue; and there was a man there which had a withered hand" (Mark 3:1).

"And when the sabbath day was come, He began to teach in the synagogue: and many hearing Him were astonished, saying, From whence hath this man these things? and what wisdom is this which is given unto Him, that even such mighty works are wrought by His hands?" (Mark 6:2).

"And Jesus entered into Jerusalem, and into the temple: and when He had looked round about upon all things, and now the eventide was come, He went out unto Bethany with the twelve. And they come to Jerusalem: and Jesus went into the temple, and began to cast out them that sold and bought in the temple, and overthrew the tables of the money-changers, and the seats of them that sold doves" (Mark 11:11,15).

"And He came by the Spirit into the temple: and when the parents brought in the child Jesus, to do for Him after the custom of the law, And it came to pass, that after three days they found Him in the temple, sitting in the midst of the doctors, both hearing them, and asking them questions. And all that heard Him were astonished at His understanding and answers. And when they saw Him, they were amazed: and His mother said unto Him, Son, why hast thou thus dealt with us? behold,

thy father and I have sought thee sorrowing. And
He said unto them, How is it that ye sought Me?
wist ye not that I must be about My Father's
business?" (Luke 2:27,46-49).

"And He came to Nazareth, where He had been
brought up: and, as His custom was, He went into
the synagogue on the sabbath day, and stood up for
to read" (Luke 4:16).

"Afterward Jesus findeth him in the temple, and
said unto him, Behold, thou art made whole: sin no
more, lest a worse thing come unto thee" (John 5:14).

"Now about the midst of the feast Jesus went
up into the temple, and taught. Then cried Jesus in
the temple as He taught, saying, Ye both know Me,
and ye know whence I am: and I am not come of
myself, but He that sent Me is true, Whom ye know
not. But I know Him: for I am from Him, and he
hath sent Me" (John 7:14,28,29).

"These words spake Jesus in the treasury, as
He taught in the temple: and no man laid hands on
Him; for His hour was not yet come" (John 8:20).

"And Jesus walked in the temple in Solomon's
porch" (John 10:23).

"Saying, Father, if thou be willing, remove this cup from Me: nevertheless not My will, but Thine, be done."

(Luke 22:42)

~ 14 ~

THE COMMITMENT OF JESUS

"The Spirit of the Lord is upon Me, because He hath anointed Me to preach the gospel to the poor; He hath sent Me to heal the brokenhearted, to preach deliverance to the captives, and recovering of sight to the blind, to set at liberty them that are bruised, To preach the acceptable year of the Lord" (Luke 4:18,19).

"And He began to say unto them, This day is this scripture fulfilled in your ears" (Luke 4:21).

"Saying, Father, if thou be willing, remove this cup from Me: nevertheless not My will, but Thine, be done" (Luke 22:42).

"And when He had made a scourge of small cords, He drove them all out of the temple, and the sheep, and the oxen; and poured out the changers' money, and overthrew the tables; And said unto them that sold doves, Take these things hence; make not My Father's house an house of merchandise" (John 2:15,16).

"But Jesus answered them, My Father worketh hitherto, and I work. I can of Mine own self do nothing: as I hear, I judge: and My judgment is just; because I seek not Mine own will, but the will of the Father which hath sent Me. But I have greater witness than that of John: for the works which the Father hath given Me to finish, the same works that I do, bear witness of Me, that the Father hath sent Me" (John 5:17,30,36).

"For I came down from heaven, not to do Mine own will, but the will of Him that sent Me. And this is the Father's will which hath sent Me, that of all which He hath given Me I should lose nothing, but should raise it up again at the last day" (John 6:38, 39).

"I have glorified Thee on the earth: I have finished the work which Thou gavest Me to do" (John 17:4).

"And yet if I judge, My judgment is true: for I am not alone, but I and the Father that sent Me. I am one that bear witness of Myself, and the Father that sent Me beareth witness of Me. I have many things to say and to judge of you: but He that sent Me is true; and I speak to the world those things which I have heard of Him" (John 8:16,18,26).

"Though He were a Son, yet learned He obedience by the things which He suffered" (Hebrews 5:8).

"Wherefore He is able also to save them to the uttermost that come unto God by Him, seeing He ever liveth to make intercession for them" (Hebrews 7:25).

"Then said I, Lo, I come (in the volume of the book it is written of Me,) to do Thy will, O God" (Hebrews 10:7).

≈ 15 ≈

THE COMPASSION OF JESUS

"But when He saw the multitudes, He was moved with compassion on them, because they fainted, and were scattered abroad, as sheep having no shepherd" (Matthew 9:36).

"And Jesus went forth, and saw a great multitude, and was moved with compassion toward them, and He healed their sick" (Matthew 14:14).

"Then Jesus called His disciples unto Him, and said, I have compassion on the multitude, because they continue with Me now three days, and have nothing to eat: and I will not send them away fasting, lest they faint in the way" (Matthew 15:32).

"So Jesus had compassion on them, and touched their eyes: and immediately their eyes received sight, and they followed Him" (Matthew 20:34).

"O Jerusalem, Jerusalem, thou that killest the prophets, and stonest them which are sent unto thee, how often would I have gathered thy children together, even as a hen gathereth her chickens under her wings, and ye would not!" (Matthew 23:37).

"And Jesus, moved with compassion, put forth His hand, and touched him, and saith unto him, I will; be thou clean" (Mark 1:41).

Howbeit Jesus suffered him not, but saith unto him, Go home to thy friends, and tell them how great things the Lord hath done for thee, and hath had compassion on thee" (Mark 5:19).

"And Jesus, when He came out, saw much people, and was moved with compassion toward them, because they were as sheep not having a shepherd: and He began to teach them many things" (Mark 6:34).

"And ofttimes it hath cast him into the fire, and into the waters, to destroy him: but if thou canst do any thing, have compassion on us, and help us" (Mark 9:22).

"And when the Lord saw her, He had compassion on her, and said unto her, Weep not" (Luke 7:13).

"Jesus wept. Then said the Jews, Behold how He loved him!" (John 11:35,36).

"Now before the feast of the passover, when Jesus knew that His hour was come that He should depart out of this world unto the Father, having loved His own which were in the world, He loved them unto the end" (John 13:1).

"As the Father hath loved Me, so have I loved you: continue ye in My love. Greater love hath no man than this, that a man lay down his life for his friends" (John 15:9,13).

"For the love of Christ constraineth us; because we thus judge, that if one died for all, then were all dead" (2 Corinthians 5:14).

"For we have not an high priest which cannot be touched with the feeling of our infirmities; but was in all points tempted like as we are, yet without sin" (Hebrews 4:15).

"Who can have compassion on the ignorant, and on them that are out of the way; for that He Himself also is compassed with infirmity" (Hebrews 5:2).

"But without faith it is impossible to please Him: for He that cometh to God must believe that He is, and that He is a rewarder of them that diligently seek Him" (Hebrews 11:6).

≈ 16 ≈

The Critics Of Jesus

"Then Peter took Him, and began to rebuke Him, saying, Be it far from Thee, Lord: this shall not be unto Thee. But He turned, and said unto Peter, Get thee behind Me, Satan: thou art an offence unto Me: for thou savourest not the things that be of God, but those that be of men" (Matthew 16:22,23).

"And when the chief priests and scribes saw the wonderful things that He did, and the children crying in the temple, and saying, Hosanna to the son of David; they were sore displeased, And said unto Him, Hearest thou what these say? And Jesus saith unto them, Yea; have ye never read, Out of the mouth of babes and sucklings thou hast perfected praise?" (Matthew 21:15,16).

"Now the chief priests, and elders, and all the council, sought false witness against Jesus, to put him to death; But found none: yea, though many false witnesses came, yet found they none. At the last came two false witnesses" (Matthew 26:59,60).

"And Judas Iscariot, one of the twelve, went unto the chief priests, to betray Him unto them. And when they heard it, they were glad, and promised to give him money. And he sought how he might conveniently betray Him" (Mark 14:10,11).

"And when He had said these things, all His adversaries were ashamed: and all the people rejoiced for all the glorious things that were done by Him" (Luke 13:17).

"And when they saw it, they all murmured, saying, That He was gone to be guest with a man that is a sinner" (Luke 19:7).

"But He perceived their craftiness, and said unto them, Why tempt ye Me? And He said unto them, Render therefore unto Caesar the things which be Caesar's, and unto God the things which be God's. And they could not take hold of His words before the people: and they marvelled at His answer, and held their peace" (Luke 20:23,25,26).

"And many other things blasphemously spake they against Him" (Luke 22:65).

"After these things Jesus walked in Galilee: for He would not walk in Jewry, because the Jews sought to kill Him. For neither did His brethren believe in Him" (John 7:1,5).

"Then took they up stones to cast at Him: but Jesus hid Himself, and went out of the temple, going through the midst of them, and so passed by" (John 8:59).

"There was a division therefore again among the Jews for these sayings. Then the Jews took up stones again to stone Him. The Jews answered Him, saying, For a good work we stone thee not; but for blasphemy; and because that Thou, being a man, makest Thyself God" (John 10:19,31,33).

"Then from that day forth they took counsel together for to put Him to death. Jesus therefore walked no more openly among the Jews; but went thence unto a country near to the wilderness, into a city called Ephraim, and there continued with His disciples" (John 11:53,54).

"And when He had thus spoken, one of the officers which stood by struck Jesus with the palm of his hand, saying, Answerest Thou the high priest so? They answered and said unto him, If He were not a malefactor, we would not have delivered Him up unto thee" (John 18:22,30).

"And from thenceforth Pilate sought to release Him: but the Jews cried out, saying, If thou let this man go, thou art not Caesar's friend: whosoever maketh himself a king speaketh against Caesar. But they cried out, Away with Him, away with Him, crucify Him. Pilate saith unto them, Shall I crucify your King? The chief priests answered, We have no king but Caesar" (John 19:12,15).

"But they cried, saying, Crucify Him, crucify Him. And they were instant with loud voices, requiring that He might be crucified. And the voices of them and of the chief priests prevailed."

(Luke 23:21,23)

≈ 17 ≈

THE CRUCIFIXION OF JESUS

"Ye know that after two days is the feast of the passover, and the Son of man is betrayed to be crucified. Then saith Jesus unto them, All ye shall be offended because of Me this night: for it is written, I will smite the shepherd, and the sheep of the flock shall be scattered abroad" (Matthew 26:2,31).

"Pilate saith unto them, What shall I do then with Jesus which is called Christ? They all say unto him, Let Him be crucified. And the governor said, Why, what evil hath He done? But they cried out the more, saying, Let Him be crucified. Then released he Barabbas unto them: and when he had scourged Jesus, he delivered Him to be crucified. And after that they had mocked Him, they took the robe off from Him, and put His own raiment on Him, and led Him away to crucify Him. And they crucified Him, and parted His garments, casting lots: that it might be fulfilled which was spoken by the prophet, They parted My garments among them, and upon My vesture did they cast lots. He saved others; Himself He cannot save. If He be the King of Israel, let Him now come down from the cross, and we will believe Him" (Matthew 27:22,23,26,31,35,42).

"And they compel one Simon a Cyrenian, who passed by, coming out of the country, the father of Alexander and Rufus, to bear His cross. And it was the third hour, and they crucified Him. And with Him they crucify two thieves; the one on His right hand, and the other on His left" (Mark 15:21,25,27).

"But they cried, saying, Crucify Him, crucify Him. And they were instant with loud voices, requiring that He might be crucified. And the voices of them and of the chief priests prevailed" (Luke 23:21,23).

"Saying, The Son of man must be delivered into the hands of sinful men, and be crucified, and the third day rise again" (Luke 24:7).

"Then said Jesus unto them, When ye have lifted up the Son of man, then shall ye know that I am He, and that I do nothing of Myself; but as My Father hath taught Me, I speak these things" (John 8:28).

"And I, if I be lifted up from the earth, will draw all men unto Me" (John 12:32).

"This He said, signifying what death He should die" (John 12:33).

"And He bearing His cross went forth into a place called the place of a skull, which is called in the Hebrew Golgotha: Where they crucified Him, and two other with Him, on either side one, and Jesus in the midst. And Pilate wrote a title, and put it on the cross. And the writing was, Jesus Of Nazareth The King Of the Jews. This title then read many of the Jews: for the place where Jesus was crucified was nigh to the city: and it was written in Hebrew, and Greek, and Latin. Now there stood by the cross of Jesus His mother, and His mother's sister, Mary the wife of Cleophas, and Mary Magdalene. But one of the soldiers with a spear pierced His side, and forthwith came there out blood and water" (John 19:17-20,25,34).

∾ 18 ∾

THE DETERMINATION OF JESUS

"And He said unto them, Let us go into the next towns, that I may preach there also: for therefore came I forth" (Mark 1:38).

"And ye shall be hated of all men for My name's sake: but he that endureth to the end shall be saved. But when they persecute you in this city, flee ye into another: for verily I say unto you, Ye shall not have gone over the cities of Israel, till the Son of man be come" (Matthew 10:22,23).

"But he that shall endure unto the end, the same shall be saved" (Matthew 24:13).

"And ye shall be hated of all men for My name's sake: but he that shall endure unto the end, the same shall be saved" (Mark 13:13).

"And it came to pass, when the time was come that He should be received up, He steadfastly set His face to go to Jerusalem" (Luke 9:51).

"And He went through the cities and villages, teaching, and journeying toward Jerusalem" (Luke 13:22).

"And when He had thus spoken, He went before, ascending up to Jerusalem" (Luke 19:28).

"And He must needs go through Samaria" (John 4:4).

"When Jesus therefore perceived that they would come and take Him by force, to make Him a king, He departed again into a mountain Himself alone" (John 6:15).

"Therefore they sought again to take Him: but He escaped out of their hand" (John 10:39).

"Then from that day forth they took counsel together for to put Him to death. Jesus therefore walked no more openly among the Jews; but went thence unto a country near to the wilderness, into a city called Ephraim, and there continued with His disciples" (John 11:53,54).

"While ye have light, believe in the light, that ye may be the children of light. These things spake Jesus, and departed, and did hide Himself from them" (John 12:36).

"Though He were a Son, yet learned He obedience by the things which He suffered" (Hebrews 5:8).

"Looking unto Jesus the author and finisher of our faith; Who for the joy that was set before Him endured the cross, despising the shame, and is set down at the right hand of the throne of God. For consider Him that endured such contradiction of sinners against Himself, lest ye be wearied and faint in your minds" (Hebrews 12:2,3).

≈ 19 ≈

THE DISAPPOINTMENTS OF JESUS

"Which when Jesus perceived, He said unto them, O ye of little faith, why reason ye among yourselves, because ye have brought no bread? Do ye not yet understand, neither remember the five loaves of the five thousand, and how many baskets ye took up? Neither the seven loaves of the four thousand, and how many baskets ye took up? How is it that ye do not understand that I spake it not to you concerning bread, that ye should beware of the leaven of the Pharisees and of the Sadducees?" (Matthew 16:8-11).

"O Jerusalem, Jerusalem, thou that killest the prophets, and stonest them which are sent unto thee, how often would I have gathered thy children together, even as a hen gathereth her chickens under her wings, and ye would not!" (Matthew 23:37).

"And as they did eat, He said, Verily I say unto you, that one of you shall betray Me. Then Judas, which betrayed Him, answered and said, Master, is it I? He said unto Him, Thou hast said. Jesus said unto him, Verily I say unto thee, That this night, before the cock crow, thou shalt deny Me thrice. And He cometh unto the disciples, and findeth them asleep, and saith unto Peter, What, could ye not watch with me one hour? And He came and found

them asleep again: for their eyes were heavy"
(Matthew 26:21,25,34,40,43).

"But Jesus said unto them, A prophet is not
without honour, but in his own country, and among
his own kin, and in his own house. And he could
there do no mighty work, save that he laid his hands
upon a few sick folk, and healed them" (Mark 6:4,5).

"Having eyes, see ye not? and having ears, hear
ye not? and do ye not remember? When I brake the
five loaves among five thousand, how many baskets
full of fragments took ye up? They say unto Him,
Twelve. And He said unto them, How is it that ye
do not understand?" (Mark 8:18,19,21).

"And He said, Verily I say unto you, No prophet
is accepted in his own country" (Luke 4:24).

"Then He said unto them, O fools, and slow of
heart to believe all that the prophets have spoken"
(Luke 24:25).

"He came unto His own, and His own received
Him not" (John 1:11).

"And ye have not His word abiding in you: for
Whom He hath sent, Him ye believe not" (John 5:38).

"But I said unto you, That ye also have seen
Me, and believe not. But there are some of you that
believe not. For Jesus knew from the beginning who
they were that believed not, and who should betray
Him. From that time many of His disciples went
back, and walked no more with Him" (John 6:36,
64,66).

"For neither did His brethren believe in Him"
(John 7:5).

≈ 20 ≈

The Disciples Of Jesus

"And He saith unto them, Follow Me, and I will make you fishers of men. And going on from thence, He saw other two brethren, James the son of Zebedee, and John his brother, in a ship with Zebedee their father, mending their nets; and He called them" (Matthew 4:19,21).

"And His disciples came to Him, and awoke Him, saying, Lord, save us: we perish" (Matthew 8:25).

"Then saith He unto His disciples, The harvest truly is plenteous, but the labourers are few" (Matthew 9:37).

"And when He had called unto Him His twelve disciples, He gave them power against unclean spirits, to cast them out, and to heal all manner of sickness and all manner of disease" (Matthew 10:1).

"And when the disciples saw Him walking on the sea, they were troubled, saying, It is a spirit; and they cried out for fear" (Matthew 14:26).

"And when His disciples were come to the other side, they had forgotten to take bread. Then Jesus said unto them, Take heed and beware of the leaven of the Pharisees and of the Sadducees. And they reasoned among themselves, saying, It is because we have taken no bread. Which when Jesus perceived, He said unto them, O ye of little faith, why reason ye among yourselves, because ye have brought no bread? Do ye not yet understand, neither remember the five loaves of the five thousand, and how many baskets ye took up? Neither the seven loaves of the four thousand, and how many baskets ye took up? How is it that ye do not understand that I spake it not to you concerning bread, that ye should beware of the leaven of the Pharisees and of the Sadducees? Then understood they how that he bade them not beware of the leaven of bread, but of the doctrine of the Pharisees and of the Sadducees. When Jesus came into the coasts of Caesarea Philippi, He asked His disciples, saying, Whom do men say that I the Son of man am? And they said, Some say that Thou art John the Baptist: some, Elias; and others, Jeremias, or one of the prophets. He saith unto them, But whom say ye that I am? And Simon Peter answered and said, Thou art the Christ, the Son of the living God. And Jesus answered and said unto him, Blessed art thou, Simon Barjona: for flesh and blood hath not revealed it unto thee, but My Father which is in heaven. And I say also unto thee, That thou art Peter, and upon this rock I will build My church; and the gates of hell shall not prevail against it. And I will give unto thee the keys of the kingdom of heaven: and whatsoever thou shalt bind on earth shall be bound in heaven: and whatsoever thou shalt loose on earth shall be loosed in heaven. Then charged He His disciples that they should tell no man that He was Jesus the Christ. From that time forth began Jesus to shew unto His disciples, how that He must go unto Jerusalem, and suffer many things of the elders and chief priests and scribes, and be killed, and be raised again the third day" (Matthew 16:5-21).

"And when the disciples heard it, they fell on their face, and were sore afraid. And I brought him to thy disciples, and they could not cure him. Then came the disciples to Jesus apart, and said, Why could not we cast him out? And Jesus said unto them, Because of your unbelief: for verily I say unto you, If ye have faith as a grain of mustard Seed, ye shall say unto this mountain, Remove hence to yonder place; and it shall remove; and nothing shall be impossible unto you" (Matthew 17:6,16,19,20).

"When His disciples heard it, they were exceedingly amazed, saying, Who then can be saved? And Jesus said unto them, Verily I say unto you, That ye which have followed Me, in the regeneration when the Son of man shall sit in the throne of His glory, ye also shall sit upon twelve thrones, judging the twelve tribes of Israel" (Matthew 19:25,28).

"And the disciples went, and did as Jesus commanded them" (Matthew 21:6).

"But when His disciples saw it, they had indignation, saying, To what purpose is this waste? And the disciples did as Jesus had appointed them; and they made ready the passover. And He cometh unto the disciples, and findeth them asleep, and saith unto Peter, What, could ye not watch with Me one hour? But all this was done, that the Scriptures of the prophets might be fulfilled. Then all the disciples forsook Him, and fled" (Matthew 26:8,19,40,56).

"Then the eleven disciples went away into Galilee, into a mountain where Jesus had appointed them" (Matthew 28:16).

"And the apostles gathered themselves together unto Jesus, and told Him all things, both what they had done, and what they had taught" (Mark 6:30).

"And the first day of unleavened bread, when they killed the passover, His disciples said unto Him, Where wilt Thou that we go and prepare that Thou mayest eat the passover? And He sendeth forth two of His disciples, and saith unto them, Go ye into the city, and there shall meet you a man bearing a pitcher of water: follow Him. And His disciples went forth, and came into the city, and found as He had said unto them: and they made ready the passover" (Mark 14:12,13,16).

"And when it was day, He called unto Him His disciples: and of them He chose twelve, Whom also He named apostles; Simon, (whom He also named Peter,) and Andrew his brother, James and John, Philip and Bartholomew, Matthew and Thomas, James the son of Alphaeus, and Simon called Zelotes, And Judas the brother of James, and Judas Iscariot, which also was the traitor" (Luke 6:13-16).

"And both Jesus was called, and His disciples, to the marriage" (John 2:2).

"These things understood not His disciples at the first: but when Jesus was glorified, then remembered they that these things were written of Him, and that they had done these things unto Him" (John 12:16).

"The other disciples therefore said unto Him, We have seen the Lord. But He said unto them, Except I shall see in His hands the print of the nails, and put my finger into the print of the nails, and thrust my hand into His side, I will not believe" (John 20:25).

~ 21 ~

THE DIVINITY OF JESUS

"Behold, a virgin shall be with child, and shall bring forth a son, and they shall call His name Emmanuel, which being interpreted is, God with us" (Matthew 1:23).

"And lo a voice from heaven, saying, This is My beloved Son, in Whom I am well pleased" (Matthew 3:17).

"And, behold, they cried out, saying, What have we to do with Thee, Jesus, Thou Son of God? art Thou come hither to torment us before the time?" (Matthew 8:29).

"Then they that were in the ship came and worshipped Him, saying, Of a truth Thou art the Son of God" (Matthew 14:33).

"While He yet spake, behold, a bright cloud overshadowed them: and behold a voice out of the cloud, which said, This is My beloved Son, in Whom I am well pleased; hear ye Him" (Matthew 17:5).

"Now when the centurion, and they that were with him, watching Jesus, saw the earthquake, and those things that were done, they feared greatly, saying, Truly this was the Son of God" (Matthew 27:54).

"But He held His peace, and answered nothing. Again the high priest asked Him, and said unto Him, Art Thou the Christ, the Son of the Blessed? And

Jesus said, I am: and ye shall see the Son of man sitting on the right hand of power, and coming in the clouds of heaven" (Mark 14:61,62).

"And when the centurion, which stood over against Him, saw that He so cried out, and gave up the ghost, he said, Truly this man was the Son of God" (Mark 15:39).

"He shall be great, and shall be called the Son of the Highest: and the Lord God shall give unto Him the throne of His father David" (Luke 1:32).

"And there came a fear on all: and they glorified God, saying, That a great prophet is risen up among us; and, That God hath visited His people" (Luke 7:16).

"When he saw Jesus, he cried out, and fell down before Him, and with a loud voice said, What have I to do with Thee, Jesus, Thou Son of God most high? I beseech Thee, torment me not" (Luke 8:28).

"In the beginning was the Word, and the Word was with God, and the Word was God. The next day John seeth Jesus coming unto him, and saith, Behold the Lamb of God, which taketh away the sin of the world" (John 1:1,29).

"For God so loved the world, that He gave His only begotten Son, that whosoever believeth in Him should not perish, but have everlasting life. He that believeth on the Son hath everlasting life: and He that believeth not the Son shall not see life; but the wrath of God abideth on Him" (John 3:16,36).

"Therefore the Jews sought the more to kill Him, because He not only had broken the sabbath, but said also that God was His Father, making Himself equal with God. That all men should honour the

Son, even as they honour the Father. He that honoureth not the Son honoureth not the Father which hath sent Him" (John 5:18,23).

"Say ye of Him, whom the Father hath sanctified, and sent into the world, Thou blasphemest; because I said, I am the Son of God?" (John 10:36).

"Jesus saith unto him, Have I been so long time with you, and yet hast thou not known Me, Philip? he that hath seen Me hath seen the Father; and how sayest thou then, Shew us the Father?" (John 14:9).

"And Thomas answered and said unto Him, My Lord and my God. But these are written, that ye might believe that Jesus is the Christ, the Son of God; and that believing ye might have life through His name" (John 20:28,31).

"Therefore let all the house of Israel know assuredly, that God hath made that same Jesus, whom ye have crucified, both Lord and Christ" (Acts 2:36).

"That if thou shalt confess with thy mouth the Lord Jesus, and shalt believe in thine heart that God hath raised Him from the dead, thou shalt be saved" (Romans 10:9).

"That at the name of Jesus every knee should bow, of things in heaven, and things in earth, and things under the earth; And that every tongue should confess that Jesus Christ is Lord, to the glory of God the Father" (Philippians 2:10,11).

"But unto the Son He saith, Thy throne, O God, is for ever and ever: a sceptre of righteousness is the sceptre of Thy kingdom" (Hebrews 1:8).

"Whosoever believeth that Jesus is the Christ

is born of God: and every one that loveth Him that begat loveth Him also that is begotten of Him" (1 John 5:1).

"And He hath on His vesture and on His thigh a name written, King Of Kings, And Lord of Lords" (Revelation 19:16).

"I am Alpha and Omega, the beginning and the end, the first and the last" (Revelation 22:13).

⁓ 22 ⁓

THE EDUCATION OF JESUS

"And Jesus went about all Galilee, teaching in their synagogues, and preaching the gospel of the kingdom, and healing all manner of sickness and all manner of disease among the people" (Matthew 4:23).

"For He taught them as one having authority, and not as the scribes" (Matthew 7:29).

"And when the sabbath day was come, He began to teach in the synagogue: and many hearing Him were astonished, saying, From whence hath this man these things? and what wisdom is this which is given unto Him, that even such mighty works are wrought by His hands? And Jesus, when He came out, saw much people, and was moved with compassion toward them, because they were as sheep not having a shepherd: and He began to teach them many things" (Mark 6:2,34).

"And the child grew, and waxed strong in spirit, filled with wisdom: and the grace of God was upon Him. And He went down with them, and came to Nazareth, and was subject unto them: but His mother kept all these sayings in her heart. And Jesus increased in wisdom and stature, and in favour with God and man" (Luke 2:40,51,52).

"And He taught in their synagogues, being glorified of all" (Luke 4:15).

"The same came to Jesus by night, and said unto Him, Rabbi, we know that Thou art a teacher come from God: for no man can do these miracles that Thou doest, except God be with him" (John 3:2).

"Now about the midst of the feast Jesus went up into the temple, and taught. And the Jews marvelled, saying, How knoweth this man letters, having never learned? Jesus answered them, and said, My doctrine is not Mine, but His that sent Me. If any man will do His will, He shall know of the doctrine, whether it be of God, or whether I speak of Myself. He that speaketh of himself seeketh his own glory: but he that seeketh His glory that sent him, the same is true, and no unrighteousness is in him. Did not Moses give you the law, and yet none of you keepeth the law? Why go ye about to kill Me?" (John 7:14-19).

"And early in the morning He came again into the temple, and all the people came unto Him; and He sat down, and taught them. I speak that which I have seen with My Father: and ye do that which ye have seen with your father" (John 8:2,38).

≈ 23 ≈

THE EMOTIONS OF JESUS

"And Jesus went into the temple of God, and cast out all them that sold and bought in the temple, and overthrew the tables of the moneychangers, and the seats of them that sold doves, And said unto them, It is written, My house shall be called the house of prayer; but ye have made it a den of thieves. And the blind and the lame came to Him in the temple; and He healed them" (Matthew 21:12-14).

"But woe unto you, scribes and Pharisees, hypocrites! for ye shut up the kingdom of heaven against men: for ye neither go in yourselves, neither suffer ye them that are entering to go in. Woe unto you, scribes and Pharisees, hypocrites! for ye devour widows' houses, and for a pretence make long prayer: therefore ye shall receive the greater damnation" (Matthew 23:13,14).

"And He took with Him Peter and the two sons of Zebedee, and began to be sorrowful and very heavy. Then saith He unto them, My soul is exceeding sorrowful, even unto death: tarry ye here, and watch with Me" (Matthew 26:37,38).

"I have compassion on the multitude, because they have now been with Me three days, and have nothing to eat" (Mark 8:2).

"Then Jesus beholding him loved him, and said unto him, One thing thou lackest: go thy way, sell whatsoever thou hast, and give to the poor, and thou shalt have treasure in heaven: and come, take up the cross, and follow Me" (Mark 10:21).

"And when He was come near, He beheld the city, and wept over it" (Luke 19:41).

"And there appeared an angel unto Him from heaven, strengthening Him. And being in an agony He prayed more earnestly: and His sweat was as it were great drops of blood falling down to the ground" (Luke 22:43,44).

"Then said Jesus, Father, forgive them; for they know not what they do. And they parted His raiment, and cast lots" (Luke 23:34).

"Now a certain man was sick, named Lazarus, of Bethany, the town of Mary and her sister Martha. (It was that Mary which anointed the Lord with ointment, and wiped His feet with her hair, whose brother Lazarus was sick.) Therefore his sisters sent unto Him, saying, Lord, behold, he whom Thou lovest is sick. When Jesus heard that, He said, This sickness is not unto death, but for the glory of God, that the Son of God might be glorified thereby. Now Jesus loved Martha, and her sister, and Lazarus. Then said Jesus unto them plainly, Lazarus is dead. And I am glad for your sakes that I was not there, to the intent ye may believe; nevertheless let us go unto him. Then when Jesus came, He found that he had lain in the grave four days already. Then Martha, as soon as she heard that Jesus was coming, went and met Him: but Mary sat still in the house. Then said Martha unto Jesus, Lord, if thou hadst been here, my brother had not died. But I know, that even now, whatsoever Thou wilt ask of God, God will give it Thee. Jesus saith unto her, Thy brother shall rise again. Martha saith unto Him, I know that he shall rise again in the resurrection at the last day. Jesus said unto her, I am the resurrection, and the life: he that believeth in Me, though he were dead, yet shall he live: And whosoever liveth and believeth in Me shall never die. Believest thou this? She saith unto Him, Yea, Lord: I believe that Thou art the Christ, the Son of God, which should come into the world. And when she had so said, she went her way, and called Mary her sister secretly, saying, The Master is come, and calleth for thee. As soon as she heard that, she arose quickly, and came unto Him. Now Jesus was not yet come into the town, but was in that place where Martha met Him. The Jews then which were with her in the house, and comforted her, when they saw Mary, that she rose up hastily and went out, followed her, saying, She goeth unto the grave to weep there. Then when Mary was come where Jesus was, and saw Him, she fell down at His feet, saying unto Him, Lord, if Thou hadst been here, my brother had not died. When Jesus therefore saw her weeping, and the Jews also weeping which came with her, He groaned in the spirit, and was troubled, And said, Where have ye laid him? They said unto Him, Lord, come and see. Jesus wept. Then said the Jews, Behold how He loved him!" (John 11:1-5, 14,15,17,20-36).

"Now before the feast of the passover, when Jesus knew that His hour was come that He should depart out of this world unto the Father, having loved His own which were in the world, He loved them unto the end. Now there was leaning on Jesus' bosom one of His disciples, whom Jesus loved" (John 13:1, 23).

"As the Father hath loved Me, so have I loved you: continue ye in My love" (John 15:9).

"And from Jesus Christ, Who is the faithful witness, and the first begotten of the dead, and the prince of the kings of the earth. Unto Him that loved us, and washed us from our sins in His own blood" (Revelation 1:5).

"Behold, I will make them of the synagogue of Satan, which say they are Jews, and are not, but do lie; behold, I will make them to come and worship before Thy feet, and to know that I have loved Thee" (Revelation 3:9).

⤳ 24 ⤳

THE ENEMIES OF JESUS

"Simon the Canaanite, and Judas Iscariot, who also betrayed Him" (Matthew 10:4).

"Then the Pharisees went out, and held a council against Him, how they might destroy Him. He that is not with Me is against Me; and he that gathereth not with Me scattereth abroad" (Matthew 12:14,30).

"And consulted that they might take Jesus by subtilty, and kill Him. And He answered and said, He that dippeth his hand with Me in the dish, the same shall betray Me. Now the chief priests, and elders, and all the council, sought false witness against Jesus, to put Him to death" (Matthew 26:4,23,59).

"Rise up, let us go; lo, he that betrayeth Me is at hand. And the chief priests and all the council sought for witness against Jesus to put Him to death; and found none. For many bare false witness against Him, but their witness agreed not together. And there arose certain, and bare false witness against Him, saying, We heard Him say, I will destroy this temple that is made with hands, and within three days I will build another made without hands. But neither so did their witness agree together. And the high priest stood up in the midst, and asked Jesus, saying, Answerest Thou nothing? what is it which these witness against Thee? Then the high priest rent His clothes, and saith, What need we any further witnesses? Ye have heard the blasphemy: what think ye? And they all condemned Him to be guilty of death" (Mark 14:42,55-60,63,64).

"And the scribes and Pharisees watched Him, whether He would heal on the sabbath day; that they might find an accusation against Him" (Luke 6:7).

"He that is not with Me is against Me: and he that gathereth not with Me scattereth" (Luke 11:23).

"But those mine enemies, which would not that I should reign over them, bring hither, and slay them before me" (Luke 19:27).

"And he promised, and sought opportunity to betray Him unto them in the absence of the multitude. And many other things blasphemously spake they against Him" (Luke 22:6,65).

"And supper being ended, the devil having now put into the heart of Judas Iscariot, Simon's son, to betray Him; For He knew who should betray Him; therefore said He, Ye are not all clean" (John 13:2, 11).

"They answered Him, Jesus of Nazareth. Jesus saith unto them, I am He. And Judas also, which betrayed Him, stood with them" (John 18:5).

"The kings of the earth stood up, and the rulers were gathered together against the Lord, and against his Christ. For of a truth against Thy holy child Jesus, Whom Thou hast anointed, both Herod, and Pontius Pilate, with the Gentiles, and the people of Israel, were gathered together" (Acts 4:26,27).

"But if it be of God, ye cannot overthrow it; lest haply ye be found even to fight against God" (Acts 5:39).

"Ye stiffnecked and uncircumcised in heart and ears, ye do always resist the Holy Ghost: as your fathers did, so do ye" (Acts 7:51).

"For He must reign, till He hath put all enemies under His feet" (1 Corinthians 15:25).

"For many walk, of whom I have told you often, and now tell you even weeping, that they are the enemies of the cross of Christ" (Philippians 3:18).

"And you, that were sometime alienated and enemies in your mind by wicked works, yet now hath He reconciled" (Colossians 1:21).

"Is not this the carpenter's son? is not His mother called Mary? and His brethren, James, and Joses, and Simon, and Judas?"   (Matthew 13:55,56)

❦ 25 ❦

THE FAMILY OF JESUS

"While He yet talked to the people, behold, His mother and His brethren stood without, desiring to speak with Him. Then one said unto Him, Behold, Thy mother and Thy brethren stand without, desiring to speak with Thee. But He answered and said unto him that told him, Who is My mother? and who are My brethren? And He stretched forth His hand toward His disciples, and said, Behold My mother and My brethren! For whosoever shall do the will of My Father which is in heaven, the same is My brother, and sister, and mother" (Matthew 12:46-50).

"Is not this the carpenter's son? is not His mother called Mary? and His brethren, James, and Joses, and Simon, and Judas?" (Matthew 13:55,56).

"There came then His brethren and His mother, and, standing without, sent unto Him, calling Him" (Mark 3:31).

"Is not this the carpenter, the son of Mary, the brother of James, and Joses, and of Juda, and Simon? and are not His sisters here with us? And they were offended at Him" (Mark 6:3).

"Then came to Him His mother and His brethren, and could not come at Him for the press. And it was told Him by certain which said, Thy mother and Thy brethren stand without, desiring to see Thee. And He answered and said unto them, My mother and My brethren are these which hear the word of God, and do it" (Luke 8:19-21).

"And the third day there was a marriage in Cana of Galilee; and the mother of Jesus was there: And both Jesus was called, and His disciples, to the marriage. And when they wanted wine, the mother of Jesus saith unto Him, They have no wine. Jesus saith unto her, Woman, what have I to do with thee? Mine hour is not yet come. His mother saith unto the servants, Whatsoever He saith unto you, do it. And there were set there six waterpots of stone, after the manner the of purifying of the Jews, containing two or three firkins apiece. Jesus saith unto them, Fill the waterpots with water. And they filled them up to the brim. And He saith unto them, Draw out now, and bear unto the governor of the feast. And they bare it. When the ruler of the feast had tasted the water that was made wine, and knew not whence it was: (but the servants which drew the water knew;) the governor of the feast called the bridegroom, And saith unto him, Every man at the beginning doth set forth good wine; and when men have well drunk, then that which is worse: but thou hast kept the good wine until now. This beginning of miracles did Jesus in Cana of Galilee, and manifested forth His glory; and His disciples believed on Him. After this He went down to Capernaum, He, and His mother, and His brethren, and His disciples: and they continued there not many days" (John 2:1-12).

"His brethren therefore said unto Him, Depart hence, and go into Judaea, that Thy disciples also may see the works that Thou doest. For neither did His brethren believe in Him. But when His brethren were gone up, then went He also up unto the feast, not openly, but as it were in secret" (John 7:3,5, 10).

✎ 26 ✎

THE FASTING OF JESUS

"Then was Jesus led up of the Spirit into the wilderness to be tempted of the devil. And when He had fasted forty days and forty nights, He was afterward an hungred. And when the tempter came to Him, he said, If Thou be the Son of God, command that these stones be made bread. But He answered and said, It is written, Man shall not live by bread alone, but by every word that proceedeth out of the mouth of God. Then the devil taketh Him up into the holy city, and setteth Him on a pinnacle of the temple, And saith unto Him, If thou be the Son of God, cast thyself down: for it is written, He shall give His angels charge concerning Thee: and in their hands they shall bear thee up, lest at any time thou dash thy foot against a stone. Jesus said unto him, It is written again, Thou shalt not tempt the Lord thy God. Again, the devil taketh Him up into an exceeding high mountain, and sheweth Him all the kingdoms of the world, and the glory of them; And saith unto Him, All these things will I give Thee, if Thou wilt fall down and worship me. Then saith Jesus unto him, Get thee hence, Satan: for it is written, Thou shalt worship the Lord thy God, and Him only shalt thou serve. Then the devil leaveth Him, and, behold, angels came and ministered unto Him" (Matthew 4:1-11).

"And when they were come to the multitude, there came to Him a certain man, kneeling down to Him, and saying, Lord, have mercy on my son: for he is lunatick, and sore vexed: for ofttimes he falleth into the fire, and oft into the water. And I brought him to Thy disciples, and they could not cure him. Then Jesus answered and said, O faithless and perverse generation, how long shall I be with you? how long shall I suffer you? bring him hither to Me. And Jesus rebuked the devil; and he departed out of him: and the child was cured from that very hour. Then came the disciples to Jesus apart, and said, Why could not we cast him out? And Jesus said unto them, Because of your unbelief: for verily I say unto you, If ye have faith as a grain of mustard Seed, ye shall say unto this mountain, Remove hence to yonder place; and it shall remove; and nothing shall be impossible unto you. Howbeit this kind goeth not out but by prayer and fasting" (Matthew 17:14-21).

"Being forty days tempted of the devil. And in those days He did eat nothing: and when they were ended, He afterward hungered" (Luke 4:2).

≈ 27 ≈

THE GENEALOGY
OF JESUS

"Therefore the Lord Himself shall give you a sign; Behold, a virgin shall conceive, and bear a son, and shall call his name Immanuel" (Isaiah 7:14).

"For unto us a child is born, unto us a son is given: and the government shall be upon His shoulder: and His name shall be called Wonderful, Counsellor, The mighty God, The everlasting Father, The Prince of Peace" (Isaiah 9:6).

"And there shall come forth a rod out of the stem of Jesse, and a Branch shall grow out of His roots" (Isaiah 11:1).

"But thou, Bethlehem Ephratah, though thou be little among the thousands of Judah, yet out of thee shall He come forth unto me that is to be ruler in Israel; whose goings forth have been from of old, from everlasting" (Micah 5:2).

"The book of the generation of Jesus Christ, the son of David, the son of Abraham. Abraham begat Isaac, and Isaac begat Jacob; and Jacob begat Judas and his brethren; And Judas begat Phares and Zara of Thamar; and Phares begat Esrom; and Esrom begat Aram; And Aram begat Aminadab; and Aminadab begat Naasson; and Naasson begat Salmon; And Salmon begat Booz of Rachab; and

Booz begat Obed of Ruth; and Obed begat Jesse; And Jesse begat David the king; and David the king begat Solomon of her that had been the wife of Urias; And Solomon begat Roboam; and Roboam begat Abia; and Abia begat Asa; And Asa begat Josaphat; and Josaphat begat Joram; and Joram begat Ozias; And Ozias begat Joatham; and Joatham begat Achaz; and Achaz begat Ezekias; And Ezekias begat Manassas; and Manassas begat Amon; and Amon begat Josias; And Josias begat Jechonias and his brethren, about the time they were carried away to Babylon: And after they were brought to Babylon, Jechonias begat Salathiel; and Salathiel begat Zorobabel; And Zorobabel begat Abiud; and Abiud begat Eliakim; and Eliakim begat Azor; And Azor begat Sadoc; and Sadoc begat Achim; and Achim begat Eliud; And Eliud begat Eleazar; and Eleazar begat Matthan; and Matthan begat Jacob; And Jacob begat Joseph the husband of Mary, of whom was born Jesus, who is called Christ. So all the generations from Abraham to David are fourteen generations; and from David until the carrying away into Babylon are fourteen generations; and from the carrying away into Babylon unto Christ are fourteen generations. Now the birth of Jesus Christ was on this wise: When as His mother Mary was espoused to Joseph, before they came together, she was found with child of the Holy Ghost. Then Joseph her husband, being a just man, and not willing to make her a publick example, was minded to put her away privily. But while he thought on these things, behold, the angel of the Lord appeared unto him in a dream, saying, Joseph, thou son of David, fear not to take unto thee Mary thy wife: for that which is conceived in her is of the Holy

Ghost. And she shall bring forth a son, and thou shalt call His name *Jesus*: for He shall save His people from their sins. Now all this was done, that it might be fulfilled which was spoken of the Lord by the prophet, saying, Behold, a virgin shall be with a child, and shall bring forth a son, and they shall call His name Emmanuel, which being interpreted is, God with us. Then Joseph being raised from sleep did as the angel of the Lord had bidden him, and took unto him his wife: And knew her not till she had brought forth her firstborn son: and he called His name *Jesus*" (Matthew 1:1-25).

"Now when Jesus was born in Bethlehem of Judaea in the days of Herod the king, behold, there came wise men from the east to Jerusalem, And thou Bethlehem, in the land of Juda, art not the least among the princes of Juda: for out of thee shall come a Governor, that shall rule My people Israel. And when they were come into the house, they saw the young child with Mary His mother, and fell down, and worshipped Him: and when they had opened their treasures, they presented unto Him gifts; gold, and frankincense, and myrrh. And when they were departed, behold, the angel of the Lord appeareth to Joseph in a dream, saying, Arise, and take the young child and His mother, and flee into Egypt, and be thou there until I bring thee word: for Herod will seek the young child to destroy Him. When he arose, he took the young child and His mother by night, and departed into Egypt: And was there until the death of Herod: that it might be fulfilled which was spoken of the Lord by the prophet, saying, Out of Egypt have I called My Son" (Matthew 2:1,6,11,13-15).

"And the angel said unto her, Fear not, Mary: for thou hast found favour with God" (Luke 1:30).

"And, behold, thou shalt conceive in thy womb, and bring forth a son, and shalt call His name *Jesus*" (Luke 1:31).

"And the angel answered and said unto her, The Holy Ghost shall come upon thee, and the power of the Highest shall overshadow thee: therefore also that holy thing which shall be born of thee shall be called the Son of God" (Luke 1:35).

"And all went to be taxed, every one into his own city. And Joseph also went up from Galilee, out of the city of Nazareth, into Judaea, unto the city of David, which is called Bethlehem; (because he was of the house and lineage of David:) To be taxed with Mary his espoused wife, being great with child. And so it was, that, while they were there, the days were accomplished that she should be delivered. But Mary kept all these things, and pondered them in her heart" (Luke 2:3-6,19).

"And Jesus Himself began to be about thirty years of age, being (as was supposed) the son of Joseph, which was the son of Heli" (Luke 3:23).

"And the Word was made flesh, and dwelt among us, (and we beheld His glory, the glory as of the only begotten of the Father,) full of grace and truth" (John 1:14).

"Concerning His Son Jesus Christ our Lord, which was made of the Seed of David according to the flesh" (Romans 1:3).

"But when the fullness of the time was come, God sent forth His Son, made of a woman, made under the law" (Galatians 4:4).

28

THE HEALING MINISTRY OF JESUS

"And Jesus went about all Galilee, teaching in their synagogues, and preaching the gospel of the kingdom, and healing all manner of sickness and all manner of disease among the people" (Matthew 4:23).

"And Jesus put forth His hand, and touched him, saying, I will; be thou clean. And immediately his leprosy was cleansed. And Jesus said unto the centurion, Go thy way; and as thou hast believed, so be it done unto thee. And his servant was healed in the selfsame hour. And He touched her hand, and the fever left her: and she arose, and ministered unto them" (Matthew 8:3,13,15).

"But when the people were put forth, He went in, and took her by the hand, and the maid arose. And Jesus went about all the cities and villages, teaching in their synagogues, and preaching the gospel of the kingdom, and healing every sickness and every disease among the people" (Matthew 9:25, 35).

"Then saith He to the man, Stretch forth thine hand. And he stretched it forth; and it was restored whole, like as the other. Then the Pharisees went out, and held a council against Him, how they might destroy Him. But when Jesus knew it, He withdrew Himself from thence: and great multitudes followed Him, and He healed them all; Then was brought unto Him one possessed with a devil, blind, and dumb: and He healed Him, insomuch that the blind and dumb both spake and saw" (Matthew 12:13-15,22).

"And Jesus went forth, and saw a great multitude, and was moved with compassion toward them, and He healed their sick. And besought Him that they might only touch the hem of His garment: and as many as touched were made perfectly whole" (Matthew 14:14,36).

"And great multitudes came unto Him, having with them those that were lame, blind, dumb, maimed, and many others, and cast them down at Jesus' feet; and He healed them" (Matthew 15:30).

"And Jesus rebuked the devil; and he departed out of him: and the child was cured from that very hour" (Matthew 17:18).

"And great multitudes followed Him; and He healed them there" (Matthew 19:2).

"And the blind and the lame came to Him in the temple; and He healed them" (Matthew 21:14).

"And He came and took her by the hand, and lifted her up; and immediately the fever left her, and she ministered unto them. And He healed many that were sick of divers diseases, and cast out many devils; and suffered not the devils to speak, because they knew Him" (Mark 1:31,34).

"For He had healed many; insomuch that they pressed upon Him for to touch him, as many as had plagues" (Mark 3:10).

"And Jesus said unto him, Go thy way; thy faith hath made thee whole. And immediately he received his sight, and followed Jesus in the way" (Mark 10:52).

"Now when the sun was setting, all they that had any sick with divers diseases brought them unto Him; and He laid His hands on every one of them, and healed them" (Luke 4:40).

"But so much the more went there a fame abroad of Him: and great multitudes came together to hear, and to be healed by Him of their infirmities" (Luke 5:15).

"And they that were vexed with unclean spirits: and they were healed" (Luke 6:18).

"And in that same hour He cured many of their infirmities and plagues, and of evil spirits; and unto many that were blind He gave sight" (Luke 7:21).

"And He laid His hands on her: and immediately she was made straight, and glorified God. And the ruler of the synagogue answered with indignation, because that Jesus had healed on the sabbath day, and said unto the people, There are six days in which men ought to work: in them therefore come and be healed, and not on the sabbath day" (Luke 13:13,14).

"And when He saw them, He said unto them, Go shew yourselves unto the priests. And it came to pass, that, as they went, they were cleansed" (Luke 17:14).

"And Jesus answered and said, Suffer ye thus far. And He touched his ear, and healed him" (Luke 22:51).

"And immediately the man was made whole, and took up his bed, and walked: and on the same day was the sabbath" (John 5:9).

"When He had thus spoken, He spat on the ground, and made clay of the spittle, and He anointed the eyes of the blind man with the clay, And said unto him, Go, wash in the pool of Siloam, (which is by interpretation, Sent.) He went his way therefore, and washed, and came seeing" (John 9:6,7).

≈ 29 ≈

THE HUMANITY OF JESUS

———————

"And there shall come forth a rod out of the stem of Jesse, and a Branch shall grow out of His roots" (Isaiah 11:1).

"As many were astonied at thee; his visage was so marred more than any man, and his form more than the sons of men" (Isaiah 52:14).

"He is despised and rejected of men; a man of sorrows, and acquainted with grief: and we hid as it were our faces from Him; He was despised, and we esteemed Him not. Surely He hath borne our griefs, and carried our sorrows: yet we did esteem Him stricken, smitten of God, and afflicted. He was oppressed, and He was afflicted, yet He opened not His mouth: He is brought as a lamb to the slaughter, and as a sheep before her shearers is dumb, so openeth not His mouth" (Isaiah 53:3,4,7).

"The book of the generation of Jesus Christ, the son of David, the son of Abraham. And Jacob begat Joseph the husband of Mary, of whom was born Jesus, Who is called Christ" (Matthew 1:1,16).

"Now when Jesus was born in Bethlehem of Judaea in the days of Herod the king, behold, there came wise men from the east to Jerusalem" (Matthew 2:1).

"And He took with Him Peter and the two sons of Zebedee, and began to be sorrowful and very heavy" (Matthew 26:37).

"And He cometh the third time, and saith unto them, Sleep on now, and take your rest: it is enough, the hour is come; behold, the Son of man is betrayed into the hands of sinners" (Mark 14:41).

"And the child grew, and waxed strong in spirit, filled with wisdom: and the grace of God was upon Him. And Jesus increased in wisdom and stature, and in favour with God and man" (Luke 2:40,52).

"And Jesus Himself began to be about thirty years of age, being (as was supposed) the son of Joseph, which was the son of Heli" (Luke 3:23).

"Being forty days tempted of the devil. And in those days He did eat nothing: and when they were ended, He afterward hungered" (Luke 4:2).

"Said unto them, Ye have brought this man unto me, as one that perverteth the people: and, behold, I, having examined Him before you, have found no fault in this man touching those things whereof ye accuse Him" (Luke 23:14).

"And the Word was made flesh, and dwelt among us, (and we beheld His glory, the glory as of the only begotten of the Father,) full of grace and truth" (John 1:14).

"He answered and said, A man that is called Jesus made clay, and anointed mine eyes, and said unto me, Go to the pool of Siloam, and wash: and I went and washed, and I received sight" (John 9:11).

"Then came Jesus forth, wearing the crown of thorns, and the purple robe. And Pilate saith unto them, Behold the man!" (John 19:5).

"And after this Joseph of Arimathaea, being a disciple of Jesus, but secretly for fear of the Jews, besought Pilate that he might take away the body of Jesus: and Pilate gave him leave. He came therefore, and took the body of Jesus. Then took they the body of Jesus, and wound it in linen clothes with the spices, as the manner of the Jews is to bury" (John 19:38,40).

"And when He had sent the multitudes away, He went up into a mountain apart to pray: and when the evening was come, He was there alone."
(Matthew 14:23)

≈ 30 ≈

THE LONELINESS OF JESUS

"And they were offended in Him. But Jesus said unto them, A prophet is not without honour, save in his own country, and in his own house. And He did not many mighty works there because of their unbelief" (Matthew 13:57,58).

"And when He had sent the multitudes away, He went up into a mountain apart to pray: and when the evening was come, He was there alone" (Matthew 14:23).

"Then cometh Jesus with them unto a place called Gethsemane, and saith unto the disciples, Sit ye here, while I go and pray yonder. And He took with Him Peter and the two sons of Zebedee, and began to be sorrowful and very heavy. Then saith He unto them, My soul is exceeding sorrowful, even unto death: tarry ye here, and watch with Me. And He cometh unto the disciples, and findeth them asleep, and saith unto Peter, What, could ye not watch with Me one hour? And He came and found them asleep again: for their eyes were heavy. But all this was done, that the scriptures of the prophets might be fulfilled. Then all the disciples forsook Him, and fled" (Matthew 26:36-40,43,56).

"And about the ninth hour Jesus cried with a

loud voice, saying, Eli, Eli, lama sabachthani? that is to say, My God, My God, why hast Thou forsaken Me?" (Matthew 27:46).

"And He said, Abba, Father, all things are possible unto Thee; take away this cup from Me: nevertheless not what I will, but what Thou wilt. And He cometh the third time, and saith unto them, Sleep on now, and take your rest: it is enough, the hour is come; behold, the Son of man is betrayed into the hands of sinners. And they all forsook Him, and fled" (Mark 14:36,41,50).

"And it came to pass, as He was alone praying, His disciples were with Him: and He asked them, saying, Whom say the people that I am? And Jesus said unto him, Foxes have holes, and birds of the air have nests; but the Son of man hath not where to lay His head" (Luke 9:18,58).

"And in the day time He was teaching in the temple; and at night He went out, and abode in the mount that is called the mount of Olives" (Luke 21:37).

"And He was withdrawn from them about a stone's cast, and kneeled down, and prayed, And there appeared an angel unto Him from heaven, strengthening Him" (Luke 22:41,43).

⟫ 31 ⟫

THE LOVE OF JESUS

"But when He saw the multitudes, He was moved with compassion on them, because they fainted, and were scattered abroad, as sheep having no shepherd" (Matthew 9:36).

"Then Jesus called His disciples unto Him, and said, I have compassion on the multitude, because they continue with Me now three days, and have nothing to eat: and I will not send them away fasting, lest they faint in the way" (Matthew 15:32).

"Then the lord of that servant was moved with compassion, and loosed him, and forgave him the debt. Shouldest not thou also have had compassion on thy fellowservant, even as I had pity on thee?" (Matthew 18:27,33).

"But Jesus said, Suffer little children, and forbid them not, to come unto Me: for of such is the kingdom of heaven" (Matthew 19:14).

"So Jesus had compassion on them, and touched their eyes: and immediately their eyes received sight, and they followed Him" (Matthew 20:34).

"Then Jesus beholding him loved him, and said unto him, One thing thou lackest: go thy way, sell whatsoever thou hast, and give to the poor, and thou shalt have treasure in heaven: and come, take up the cross, and follow Me" (Mark 10:21).

"And when the Lord saw her, He had compassion

on her, and said unto her, Weep not" (Luke 7:13).

"But a certain Samaritan, as he journeyed, came where he was: and when he saw him, he had compassion on him, And went to him, and bound up his wounds, pouring in oil and wine, and set him on his own beast, and brought him to an inn, and took care of him. And on the morrow when he departed, he took out two pence, and gave them to the host, and said unto him, Take care of him; and whatsoever thou spendest more, when I come again, I will repay thee" (Luke 10:33-35).

"For God so loved the world, that He gave His only begotten son, that whosoever believeth in Him should not perish, but have everlasting life" (John 3:16).

"As the Father hath loved Me, so have I loved you: continue ye in My love. This is My command-ment, That ye love one another, as I have loved you" (John 15:9,12).

"And walk in love, as Christ also hath loved us, and hath given Himself for us an offering and a sacrifice to God for a sweetsmelling savour. But fornication, and all uncleanness, or covetousness, let it not be once named among you, as becometh saints" (Ephesians 5:2,3).

"We love Him, because He first loved us" (1 John 4:19).

"And from Jesus Christ, Who is the faithful witness, and the first begotten of the dead, and the prince of the kings of the earth. Unto Him that loved us, and washed us from our sins in His own blood" (Revelation 1:5).

~ 32 ~

THE MINISTRY OF JESUS

"Behold My servant, whom I uphold; Mine elect, in whom My soul delighteth; I have put My Spirit upon him: he shall bring forth judgment to the Gentiles" (Isaiah 42:1).

"The Spirit of the Lord God is upon me; because the Lord hath anointed me to preach good tidings unto the meek; he hath sent me to bind up the brokenhearted, to proclaim liberty to the captives, and the opening of the prison to them that are bound; To proclaim the acceptable year of the Lord, and the day of vengeance of our God; to comfort all that mourn; To appoint unto them that mourn in Zion, to give unto them beauty for ashes, the oil of joy for mourning, the garment of praise for the spirit of heaviness; that they might be called trees of righteousness, the planting of the Lord, that He might be glorified" (Isaiah 61:1-3).

"From that time Jesus began to preach, and to say, Repent: for the kingdom of heaven is at hand. And Jesus went about all Galilee, teaching in their synagogues, and preaching the gospel of the kingdom, and healing all manner of sickness and all manner of disease among the people" (Matthew 4:17,23).

"And Jesus went about all the cities and villages, teaching in their synagogues, and preaching the gospel of the kingdom, and healing every sickness and every disease among the people" (Matthew 9:35).

"And it came to pass, when Jesus had made an end of commanding His twelve disciples, He departed thence to teach and to preach in their cities" (Matthew 11:1).

"And when He was come into His own country, He taught them in their synagogue, insomuch that they were astonished, and said, Whence hath this man this wisdom, and these mighty works? And He did not many mighty works there because of their unbelief" (Matthew 13:54,58).

"Even as the Son of man came not to be ministered unto, but to minister, and to give His life a ransom for many" (Matthew 20:28).

"Now after that John was put in prison, Jesus came into Galilee, preaching the gospel of the kingdom of God. And saying, The time is fulfilled, and the kingdom of God is at hand: repent ye, and believe the gospel. And they went into Capernaum; and straightway on the sabbath day He entered into the synagogue, and taught. And they were astonished at His doctrine: for He taught them as one that had authority, and not as the scribes. And they were all amazed, insomuch that they questioned among themselves, saying, What thing is this? what new doctrine is this? for with authority commandeth He even the unclean spirits, and they do obey Him. And He preached in their synagogues throughout all Galilee, and cast out devils" (Mark 1:14,15,21, 22,27,39).

"And He ordained twelve, that they should be

with Him, and that He might send them forth to preach" (Mark 3:14).

"And Jesus answered and said, while He taught in the temple, How say the scribes that Christ is the son of David?" (Mark 12:35).

"And He taught in their synagogues, being glorified of all. And He preached in the synagogues of Galilee" (Luke 4:15,44).

"I came not to call the righteous, but sinners to repentance" (Luke 5:32).

"After these things the Lord appointed other seventy also, and sent them two and two before His face into every city and place, whither He Himself would come" (Luke 10:1).

"For I came down from heaven, not to do Mine own will, but the will of Him that sent Me" (John 6:38).

"I must work the works of Him that sent Me, while it is day: the night cometh, when no man can work. And Jesus said, For judgment I am come into this world, that they which see not might see; and that they which see might be made blind" (John 9:4,39).

"The thief cometh not, but for to steal, and to kill, and to destroy: I am come that they might have life, and that they might have it more abundantly" (John 10:10).

"I am come a light into the world, that whosoever believeth on Me should not abide in darkness" (John 12:46).

"This is a faithful saying, and worthy of all acceptation, that Christ Jesus came into the world to save sinners; of whom I am chief" (1 Timothy 1:15).

"Now of the things which we have spoken this is the sum: We have such an high priest, who is set on the right hand of the throne of the Majesty in the heavens; A minister of the sanctuary, and of the true tabernacle, which the Lord pitched, and not man" (Hebrews 8:1,2).

∞ 33 ∞

THE MIRACLES OF JESUS

"And Jesus put forth His hand, and touched Him, saying, I will; be thou clean. And immediately his leprosy was cleansed" (Matthew 8:3).

"And He saith unto them, Why are ye fearful, O ye of little faith? Then He arose, and rebuked the winds and the sea; and there was a great calm" (Matthew 8:26).

"And, behold, they brought to Him a man sick of the palsy, lying on a bed: and Jesus seeing their faith said unto the sick of the palsy; Son, be of good cheer; thy sins be forgiven thee. And, behold, a woman, which was diseased with an issue of blood twelve years, came behind Him, and touched the hem of His garment" (Matthew 9:2,20).

"Then was brought unto Him one possessed with a devil, blind, and dumb: and He healed him, insomuch that the blind and dumb both spake and saw" (Matthew 12:22).

"And in the fourth watch of the night Jesus went unto them, walking on the sea" (Matthew 14:25).

"And Jesus rebuked the devil; and he departed out of him: and the child was cured from that very hour. Notwithstanding, lest we should offend them, go thou to the sea, and cast an hook, and take up the fish that first cometh up; and when thou hast opened his mouth, thou shalt find a piece of money: that take, and give unto them for Me and thee" (Matthew 17:18,27).

"So Jesus had compassion on them, and touched their eyes: and immediately their eyes received sight, and they followed Him" (Matthew 20:34).

"And when He saw a fig tree in the way, He came to it, and found nothing thereon, but leaves only, and said unto it, Let no fruit grow on thee henceforward for ever. And presently the fig tree withered away" (Matthew 21:19).

"And He came and took her by the hand, and lifted her up; and immediately the fever left her, and she ministered unto them" (Mark 1:31).

"And Jesus, moved with compassion, put forth His hand, and touched him, and saith unto him, I will; be thou clean" (Mark 1:41).

"While He yet spake, there came from the ruler of the synagogue's house certain which said, Thy daughter is dead: why troublest thou the Master any further? As soon as Jesus heard the word that was spoken, He saith unto the ruler of the synagogue, Be not afraid, only believe. And He suffered no man to follow Him, save Peter, and James, and John the brother of James. And He cometh to the house of the ruler of the synagogue, and seeth the tumult, and them that wept and wailed greatly. And when He was come in, He saith unto them, Why make ye this ado, and weep? the damsel is not dead, but sleepeth. And they laughed Him to scorn. But when He had put them all out, He taketh the father and the mother of the damsel, and them that were with Him, and entereth in where the damsel was lying. And He took the damsel by the hand, and said unto her, Talitha cumi; which is, being interpreted, Damsel, I say unto thee, arise. And straightway the damsel arose, and walked; for she was of the age of twelve years. And they were astonished with a great astonishment" (Mark 5:35-42).

"And straightway his ears were opened, and the string of his tongue was loosed, and he spake plain" (Mark 7:35).

"But Jesus took him by the hand, and lifted him up; and he arose" (Mark 9:27).

"And as he was yet a coming, the devil threw him down, and tare him. And Jesus rebuked the unclean spirit, and healed the child, and delivered him again to his father" (Luke 9:42).

"And when Jesus saw her, He called her to Him, and said unto her, Woman, thou art loosed from thine infirmity. And He laid his hands on her: and immediately she was made straight, and glorified God" (Luke 13:12,13).

"And He saw them, He said unto them, Go shew yourselves unto the priests. And it came to pass, that, as they went, they were cleansed" (Luke 17:14).

"And when He rose up from prayer, and was come to His disciples, He found them sleeping for sorrow, And said unto them, Why sleep ye? rise and pray, lest ye enter into temptation. And while He yet spake, behold a multitude, and he that was called Judas, one of the twelve, went before them, and drew near unto Jesus to kiss Him. But Jesus said unto him, Judas, betrayest thou the son of man with a kiss? When they which were about Him saw what would follow, they said unto Him, Lord, shall we smite with the sword? And one of them smote the servant of the high priest, and cut off his right ear. And Jesus answered and said, Suffer ye thus far. And he touched his ear, and healed him" (Luke 22:45-51).

"And the third day there was a marriage in Cana of Galilee; and the mother of Jesus was there: And both Jesus was called, and His disciples, to the marriage. And when they wanted wine, the mother of Jesus saith unto him, They have no wine. Jesus saith unto her, Woman, what have I to do with thee? mine hour is not yet come. His mother saith unto the servants, Whatsoever He saith unto you, do it. And there were set there six waterpots of stone, after the manner of the purifying of the Jews, containing two or three firkins apiece. Jesus saith unto them, Fill the waterpots with water. And they filled them up to the brim. And He saith unto them, Draw out now, and bear unto the governor of the feast. And they bare it. When the ruler of the feast had tasted the water that was made wine, and knew not whence it was: (but the servants which drew the water knew;) the governor of the feast called the bridegroom" (John 2:1-9).

"And when He thus had spoken, he cried with a loud voice, Lazarus, come forth. And he that was dead came forth, bound hand and foot with graveclothes: and his face was bound about with a napkin. Jesus saith unto them, Loose him, and let him go" (John 11:43,44).

~ 34 ~

THE MISSION OF JESUS

"The Spirit of the Lord God is upon Me; because the Lord hath anointed Me to preach good tidings unto the meek; He hath sent Me to bind up the brokenhearted, to proclaim liberty to the captives, and the opening of the prison to them that are bound; To proclaim the acceptable year of the Lord, and the day of vengeance of our God; to comfort all that mourn; To appoint unto them that mourn in Zion, to give unto them beauty for ashes, the oil of joy for mourning, the garment of praise for the spirit of heaviness; that they might be called trees of righteousness, the planting of the Lord, that He might be glorified" (Isaiah 61:1-3).

"And she shall bring forth a son, and thou shalt call His name Jesus: for He shall save His people from their sins" (Matthew 1:21).

"Think not that I am come to destroy the law, or the prophets: I am not come to destroy, but to fulfil" (Matthew 5:17).

"But go ye and learn what that meaneth, I will have mercy, and not sacrifice: for I am not come to call the righteous, but sinners to repentance" (Matthew 9:13).

"Think not that I am come to send peace on earth: I came not to send peace, but a sword. For I am come to set a man at variance against his father, and the daughter against her mother, and the daughter in law against her mother in law" (Matthew 10:34,35).

"For the Son of man is come to save that which was lost" (Matthew 18:11).

"Even as the Son of man came not to be ministered unto, but to minister, and to give His life a ransom for many" (Matthew 20:28).

"Now after that John was put in prison, Jesus came into Galilee, preaching the gospel of the kingdom of God" (Mark 1:14).

"When Jesus heard it, He saith unto them, They that are whole have no need of the physician, but they that are sick: I came not to call the righteous, but sinners to repentance" (Mark 2:17).

"And He said unto them, I must preach the kingdom of God to other cities also: for therefore am I sent" (Luke 4:43).

"For the Son of man is not come to destroy men's lives, but to save them. And they went to another village" (Luke 9:56).

"After these things the Lord appointed other seventy also, and sent them two and two before His face into every city and place, whither He Himself would come" (Luke 10:1).

"I am come to send fire on the earth; and what will I, if it be already kindled?" (Luke 12:49).

"For God sent not His Son into the world to condemn the world; but that the world through Him might be saved" (John 3:17).

"And Jesus said, For judgment I am come into this world, that they which see not might see; and that they which see might be made blind" (John 9:39).

"The thief cometh not, but for to steal, and to kill, and to destroy: I am come that they might have life, and that they might have it more abundantly" (John 10:10).

"Now is My soul troubled; and what shall I say? Father, save Me from this hour: but for this cause came I unto this hour. I am come a light into the world, that whosoever believeth on Me should not abide in darkness. And if any man hear My words, and believe not, I judge him not: for I came not to judge the world, but to save the world" (John 12:27, 46,47).

"Now before the feast of the passover, when Jesus knew that His hour was come that He should depart out of this world unto the Father, having loved His own which were in the world, He loved them unto the end" (John 13:1).

"Pilate therefore said unto Him, Art thou a king then? Jesus answered, Thou sayest that I am a king. To this end was I born, and for this cause came I into the world, that I should bear witness unto the truth. Every one that is of the truth heareth My voice" (John 18:37).

"For He hath made Him to be sin for us, who knew no sin; that we might be made the righteousness of God in Him."

(2 Corinthians 5:21)

≈ 35 ≈

THE MISTAKES OF JESUS

"For He hath made Him to be sin for us, who knew no sin; that we might be made the righteousness of God in Him" (2 Corinthians 5:21).

"For unto us a child is born, unto us a son is given: and the government shall be upon His shoulder: and His name shall be called Wonderful, Counsellor, The mighty God, The everlasting Father, The Prince of Peace. Of the increase of His government and peace there shall be no end, upon the throne of David, and upon His kingdom, to order it, and to establish it with judgment and with justice from henceforth even for ever. The zeal of the Lord of hosts will perform this."

(Isaiah 9:6,7)

≈ 36 ≈

THE NAMES AND TITLES OF JESUS

"For unto us a child is born, unto us a son is given: and the government shall be upon His shoulder: and His name shall be called Wonderful, Counsellor, The mighty God, The everlasting Father, The Prince of Peace. Of the increase of His government and peace there shall be no end, upon the throne of David, and upon His kingdom, to order it, and to establish it with judgment and with justice from henceforth even for ever. The zeal of the Lord of hosts will perform this" (Isaiah 9:6,7).

"And she shall bring forth a son, and thou shalt call His name *Jesus:* for He shall save His people from their sins" (Matthew 1:21).

"Saying, Where is He that is born King of the Jews? for we have seen His star in the east, and are come to worship Him. And thou Bethlehem, in the land of Juda, art not the least among the princes of Juda; for out of thee shall come a Governor, that shall rule my people Israel. And was there until the death of Herod: that it might be fulfilled which was spoken of the Lord by the prophet, saying, Out of Egypt have I called My son. And He came and dwelt in a city called Nazareth: that it might be fulfilled which was spoken by the prophets, He shall be called a Nazarene" (Matthew 2:2,6,15,23).

"And Jesus saith unto him, The foxes have holes, and the birds of the air have nests; but the Son of man hath not where to lay His head" (Matthew 8:20).

"And the multitude said, This is Jesus the prophet of Nazareth of Galilee" (Matthew 21:11).

"He shall be great, and shall be called the Son of the Highest: and the Lord God shall give unto Him the throne of His father David: And hath raised up an horn of salvation for us in the house of His servant David; Through the tender mercy of our God; whereby the dayspring from on high hath visited us" (Luke 1:32,69,78).

"For unto you is born this day in the city of David a Saviour, which is Christ the Lord" (Luke 2:11).

"That was the true Light, which lighteth every man that cometh into the world. The next day John seeth Jesus coming unto him, and saith, Behold the Lamb of God, which taketh away the sin of the world. He first findeth his own brother Simon, and saith unto him, We have found the Messias, which is, being interpreted, the Christ" (John 1:9,29,41).

"Then spake Jesus again unto them, saying, I am the light of the world: he that followeth Me shall not walk in darkness, but shall have the light of life" (John 8:12).

"Then said Jesus unto them again, Verily, verily, I say unto you, I am the door of the sheep. I am the good shepherd: the good shepherd giveth his life for the sheep" (John 10:7,11).

"Jesus said unto her, I am the resurrection, and the life: he that believeth in Me, though he were dead, yet shall he live" (John 11:25).

"Jesus saith unto him, I am the way, the truth, and the life: no man cometh unto the Father, but by

Me" (John 14:6).

"I am the true vine, and My Father is the husbandman" (John 15:1).

"And Thomas answered and said unto him, My Lord and my God" (John 20:28).

"But ye denied the Holy One and the Just, and desired a murderer to be granted unto you; And killed the Prince of life, whom God hath raised from the dead; whereof we are witnesses" (Acts 3:14,15).

"And so it is written, The first man Adam was made a living soul; the last Adam was made a quickening spirit" (1 Corinthians 15:45).

"For there is one God, and one mediator between God and men, the man Christ Jesus" (1 Timothy 2:5).

"And from Jesus Christ, Who is the faithful witness, and the first begotten of the dead, and the prince of the kings of the earth. Unto Him that loved us, and washed us from our sins in His own blood. I am Alpha and Omega, the beginning and the ending, saith the Lord, which is, and which was, and which is to come, the Almighty. And when I saw Him, I fell at His feet as dead. And He laid His right hand upon me, saying unto me, Fear not; I am the first and the last" (Revelation 1:5,8,17).

"And one of the elders saith unto me, Weep not: behold, the Lion of the tribe of Juda, the Root of David, hath prevailed to open the book, and to loose the seven seals thereof" (Revelation 5:5).

"I Jesus have sent Mine angel to testify unto you these things in the churches. I am the root and the offspring of David, and the bright and morning star" (Revelation 22:16).

"And He went a little farther, and fell on His face, and prayed, saying, O My Father, if it be possible, let this cup pass from Me: nevertheless not as I will, but as thou wilt. He went away again the second time, and prayed, saying, O My Father, if this cup may not pass away from Me, except I drink it, Thy will be done."   (Matthew 26:39,42)

~ 37 ~

THE OBEDIENCE OF JESUS

"And lo a voice from heaven, saying, This is my beloved Son, in whom I am well pleased" (Matthew 3:17).

"Thy kingdom come. Thy will be done in earth, as it is in heaven" (Matthew 6:10).

"Not every one that saith unto Me, Lord, Lord, shall enter into the kingdom of heaven; but he that doeth the will of My Father which is in heaven" (Matthew 7:21).

"And He went a little farther, and fell on His face, and prayed, saying, O My Father, if it be possible, let this cup pass from Me: nevertheless not as I will, but as thou wilt. He went away again the second time, and prayed, saying, O My Father, if this cup may not pass away from Me, except I drink it, Thy will be done" (Matthew 26:39,42).

"And He said, Abba, Father, all things are possible unto Thee; take away this cup from Me: nevertheless not what I will, but what Thou wilt" (Mark 14:36).

"And the Holy Ghost descended in a bodily shape like a dove upon Him, and a voice came from heaven, which said, Thou art My beloved Son; in Thee I am well pleased" (Luke 3:22).

"Jesus saith unto them, My meat is to do the will of Him that sent Me, and to finish His work" (John 4:34).

"I can of Mine own self do nothing: as I hear, I judge: and My judgment is just; because I seek not Mine own will, but the will of the Father which hath sent Me. But I have greater witness than that of John: for the works which the Father hath given Me to finish, the same works that I do, bear witness of Me, that the Father hath sent Me" (John 5:30,36).

"For I came down from heaven, not to do Mine own will, but the will of Him that sent Me. And this is the Father's will which hath sent Me, that of all which He hath given Me I should lose nothing, but should raise it up again at the last day. And this is the will of Him that sent Me, that every one which seeth the Son, and believeth on Him, may have everlasting life: and I will raise Him up at the last day" (John 6:38-40).

"Jesus answered them, and said, My doctrine is not Mine, but His that sent Me" (John 7:16).

"I must work the works of Him that sent Me, while it is day: the night cometh, when no man can work" (John 9:4).

"For I have not spoken of Myself; but the Father which sent Me, He gave Me a commandment, what I should say, and what I should speak" (John 12:49).

"I have glorified Thee on the earth: I have finished the work which Thou gavest Me to do. I have manifested Thy name unto the men, which Thou gavest Me out of the world: Thine they were, and Thou gavest them Me; and they have kept Thy word. For I have given unto them the words which Thou gavest Me; and they have received them, and have known surely that I came out from Thee, and they have believed that Thou didst send Me" (John 17:4,6,8).

"Though He were a Son, yet learned He obedience by the things which He suffered" (Hebrews 5:8).

"For as by one man's disobedience many were made sinners, so by the obedience of One shall many be made righteous" (Romans 5:19).

"Surely He hath borne our griefs, and carried our sorrows: yet we did esteem Him stricken, smitten of God, and afflicted."   (Isaiah 53:4)

≈ 38 ≈

THE PAIN OF JESUS

"Surely He hath borne our griefs, and carried our sorrows: yet we did esteem Him stricken, smitten of God, and afflicted" (Isaiah 53:4).

"Then did they spit in His face, and buffeted Him; and others smote Him with the palms of their hands" (Matthew 26:67).

"And the governor said, Why, what evil hath He done? But they cried out the more, saying, Let Him be crucified. Then released he Barabbas unto them: and when he had scourged Jesus, he delivered Him to be crucified. And when they had platted a crown of thorns, they put it upon His head, and a reed in His right hand: and they bowed the knee before Him, and mocked Him, saying, Hail, King of the Jews! And they spit upon Him, and took the reed, and smote Him on the head. And they crucified Him, and parted His garments, casting lots: that it might be fulfilled which was spoken by the prophet, They parted My garments among them, and upon My vesture did they cast lots" (Matthew 27:23,26,29, 30,35).

"And saith unto them, My soul is exceeding sorrowful unto death: tarry ye here, and watch. And some began to spit on Him, and to cover His face, and to buffet Him, and to say unto Him, Prophesy: and the servants did strike Him with the palms of their hands" (Mark 14:34,65).

"And they smote Him on the head with a reed, and did spit upon Him, and bowing their knees worshipped Him" (Mark 15:19).

"And while He yet spake, behold a multitude, and he that was called Judas, one of the twelve, went before them, and drew near unto Jesus to kiss Him. But Jesus said unto him, Judas, betrayest thou the Son of man with a kiss? When they which were about Him saw what would follow, they said unto Him, Lord, shall we smite with the sword? And when they had blindfolded Him, they struck Him on the face, and asked Him, saying, Prophesy, who is it that smote Thee?" (Luke 22:47-49,64).

"Then Pilate therefore took Jesus, and scourged Him. And the soldiers platted a crown of thorns, and put it on His head, and they put on Him a purple robe, And said, Hail, King of the Jews! and they smote Him with their hands. Then came Jesus forth, wearing the crown of thorns, and the purple robe. And Pilate saith unto them, Behold the man! When the chief priests therefore and officers saw Him, the cried out, saying, Crucify Him, crucify Him. Pilate saith unto them, Take ye Him, and crucify Him: for I find no fault in Him. And He bearing His cross went forth into a place called the place of a skull, which is called in the Hebrew Golgotha: Then came the soldiers, and brake the legs of the first, and of the other which was crucified with Him. But when they came to Jesus, and saw that He was dead already, they brake not His legs: But one of the soldiers with a spear pierced His side, and forthwith came there out blood and water" (John 19:1-3,5,6,17,32-34).

～ 39 ～

THE PARABLES OF JESUS

"And He spake many things unto them in parables, saying, Behold, a sower went forth to sow; Another parable put He forth unto them, saying, The kingdom of heaven is likened unto a man which sowed good Seed in his field: Another parable put He forth unto them, saying, The Kingdom of heaven is like to a grain of mustard Seed, which a man took, and sowed in his field: Another parable spake He unto them; The kingdom of heaven is like unto leaven, which a woman took, and hid in three measures of meal, till the whole was leavened. Again, the kingdom of heaven is like unto treasure hid in a field; the which when a man hath found, he hideth, and for joy thereof goeth and selleth all that he hath, and buyeth that field. Again, the kingdom of heaven is like unto a merchant man, seeking goodly pearls: Who, when he had found one pearl of great price, went and sold all that he had, and bought it. Again, the kingdom of heaven is like unto a net, that was cast into the sea, and gathered of every kind" (Matthew 13:3,24,31,33,44-47).

"For the kingdom of heaven is like unto a man that is an householder, which went out early in the morning to hire labourers into his vineyard" (Matthew 20:1).

"Hear another parable: There was a certain

householder, which planted a vineyard, and hedged it round about, and digged a winepress in it, and built a tower, and let it out to husbandmen, and went into a far country" (Matthew 21:33).

"And Jesus answered and spake unto them again by parables, and said, The kingdom of heaven is like unto a certain king, which made a marriage for his son" (Matthew 22:1,2).

"Then shall the kingdom of heaven be likened unto ten virgins, which took their lamps, and went forth to meet the bridegroom. For the kingdom of heaven is as a man travelling into a far country, who called his own servants, and delivered unto them his goods" (Matthew 25:1,14).

"And He said unto them, Know ye not this parable? and how then will ye know all parables? The sower soweth the word. But without a parable spake He not unto them: and when they were alone, He expounded all things to His disciples" (Mark 4:13, 14,34).

"And He began to speak unto them by parables. A certain man planted a vineyard, and set an hedge about it, and digged a place for the winefat, and built a tower, and let it out to husbandmen, and went into a far country" (Mark 12:1).

"And His disciples asked Him, saying, What might this parable be? And He said, Unto you it is given to know the mysteries of the kingdom of God: but to others in parables; that seeing they might not see, and hearing they might not understand. Now the parable is this: The Seed is the word of God" (Luke 8:9-11).

"And He spake a parable unto them, saying, The

ground of a certain rich man brought forth plentifully" (Luke 12:16).

"He spake also this parable; A certain man had a fig tree planted in his vineyard; and he came and sought fruit thereon, and found none. Then said he, Unto what is the kingdom of God like? and whereunto shall I resemble it? It is like leaven, which a women took and hid in three measures of meal, till the whole was leavened" (Luke 13:6,18,21).

"And He spake this parable unto them, saying, What man of you, having an hundred sheep, if he lose one of them, doth not leave the ninety and nine in the wilderness, and go after that which is lost, until he find it?" (Luke 15:3,4).

"And He spake a parable unto them to this end, that men ought always to pray, and not to faint; And He spake this parable unto certain which trusted in themselves that they were righteous, and despised others" (Luke 18:1,9).

"And as they heard these things, He added and spake a parable, because he was nigh to Jerusalem, and because they thought that the kingdom of God should immediately appear" (Luke 19:11).

"Then began He to speak to the people this parable; A certain man planted a vineyard, and let it forth to husbandmen, and went into a far country for a long time" (Luke 20:9).

"And when they were come into the house, they saw the young child with Mary His mother, and fell down, and worshipped Him: and when they had opened their treasures, they presented unto Him gifts; gold, and frankincense, and myrrh."   (Matthew 2:11)

~ 40 ~

THE PARENTS OF JESUS

—————➤●⊄—————

"And Jacob begat Joseph the husband of Mary, of whom was born Jesus, Who is called Christ. Now the birth of Jesus Christ was on this wise: When as His mother Mary was espoused to Joseph, before they came together, she was found with child of the Holy Ghost. Then Joseph her husband, being a just man, and not willing to make her a publick example, was minded to put her away privily. But while he thought on these things, behold, the angel of the Lord appeared unto him in a dream, saying, Joseph, thou son of David, fear not to take unto thee Mary thy wife: for that which is conceived in her is of the Holy Ghost. Then Joseph being raised from sleep did as the angel of the Lord had bidden him, and took unto him his wife" (Matthew 1:16,18-20,24).

"And when they were come into the house, they saw the young child with Mary His mother, and fell down, and worshipped Him: and when they had opened their treasures, they presented unto Him gifts; gold, and frankincense, and myrrh" (Matthew 2:11).

"While He yet talked to the people, behold, His mother and His brethren stood without, desiring to speak with Him" (Matthew 12:46).

"Is not this the carpenter's son? is not His mother called Mary? and His brethren, James, and

Joses, and Simon, and Judas?" (Matthew 13:55).

"There came then His brethren and His mother, and, standing without, sent unto Him, calling Him" (Mark 3:31).

"And the angel said unto her, Fear not, Mary: for thou hast found favour with God" (Luke 1:30).

"And Mary said, Behold the handmaid of the Lord; be it unto me according to thy word. And the angel departed from her. And Mary arose in those days, and went into the hill country with haste, into a city of Juda; And entered into the house of Zacharias, and saluted Elisabeth. And whence is this to me, that the mother of my Lord should come to me? And Mary said, My soul doth magnify the Lord, And Mary abode with her about three months, and returned to her own house" (Luke 1:38-40,43,46,56).

"But Mary kept all these things, and pondered them in her heart. Now His parents went to Jerusalem every year at the feast of the passover. And He said unto them, How is it that ye sought Me? wist ye not that I must be about My Father's business? And He went down with them, and came to Nazareth, and was subject unto them: but His mother kept all these sayings in her heart" (Luke 2:19,41,49,51).

"Then came to Him His mother and His brethren, and could not come at Him for the press" (Luke 8:19).

"And the third day there was a marriage in Cana of Galilee; and the mother of Jesus was there: His mother saith unto the servants, Whatsoever He saith unto you, do it. After this He went down to

Capernaum, He, and His mother, and His brethren, and His disciples: and they continued there not many days" (John 2:1,5,12).

"Now there stood by the cross of Jesus His mother, and His mother's sister, Mary the wife of Cleophas, and Mary Magdalene" (John 19:25).

"These all continued with one accord in prayer and supplication, with the women, and Mary the mother of Jesus, and with His brethren" (Acts 1:14).

"And Jesus saith unto him, The foxes have holes, and the birds of the air have nests; but the Son of man hath not where to lay His head."   (Matthew 8:20)

～ 41 ～

THE POSSESSIONS OF JESUS

"And Jesus saith unto him, The foxes have holes, and the birds of the air have nests; but the Son of man hath not where to lay His head" (Matthew 8:20).

"And they crucified Him, and parted His garments, casting lots: that it might be fulfilled which was spoken by the prophet, They parted My garments among them, and upon My vesture did they cast lots" (Matthew 27:35).

"And when they had mocked Him, they took off the purple from Him, and put His own clothes on Him, and led Him out to crucify Him" (Mark 15:20).

"And certain women, which had been healed of evil spirits and infirmities, Mary called Magdalene, out of whom went seven devils, And Joanna the wife of Chuza Herod's steward, and Susanna, and many others, which ministered unto Him of their substance" (Luke 8:2,3).

"And Jesus said unto him, Foxes have holes, and birds of the air have nests; but the Son of man hath not where to lay His head" (Luke 9:58).

"Then said Jesus, Father, forgive them; for they know not what they do. And they parted His raiment, and cast lots" (Luke 23:34).

"Then the soldiers, when they had crucified

Jesus, took His garments, and made four parts, to
every soldier a part; and also His coat: now the coat
was without seam, woven from the top throughout.
They said therefore among themselves, Let us not
rend it, but cast lots for it, whose it shall be: that
the scripture might be fulfilled, which saith, They
parted My raiment among them, and for My vesture
they did cast lots. These things therefore the soldiers
did" (John 19:23,24).

"For ye know the grace of our Lord Jesus Christ,
that, though He was rich, yet for your sakes He
became poor, that ye through His poverty might be
rich" (2 Corinthians 8:9).

≈ 42 ≈

THE POWER OF JESUS OVER DEMONS

"But He answered and said, It is written, Man shall not live by bread alone, but by every word that proceedeth out of the mouth of God. Jesus said unto him, It is written again, Thou shalt not tempt the Lord thy God. Then saith Jesus unto him, Get thee hence, Satan: for it is written, Thou shalt worship the Lord thy God, and Him only shalt thou serve" (Matthew 4:4,7,10).

"And, behold, they cried out, saying, What have we to do with Thee, Jesus, Thou Son of God? art Thou come hither to torment us before the time? So the devils besought Him, saying, If thou cast us out, suffer us to go away into the herd of swine. And He said unto them, Go. And when they were come out, they went into the herd of swine: and, behold, the whole herd of swine ran violently down a steep place into the sea, and perished in the waters" (Matthew 8:29,31,32).

"And when the devil was cast out, the dumb spake: and the multitudes marvelled saying, It was never so seen in Israel" (Matthew 9:33).

"And when He had called unto Him His twelve disciples, He gave them power against unclean spirits, to cast them out, and to heal all manner of sickness and all manner of disease" (Matthew 10:1).

"But He turned, and said unto Peter, Get thee behind Me, Satan: thou art an offence unto Me: for thou savourest not the things that be of God, but those that be of men" (Matthew 16:23).

"And Jesus rebuked the devil; and he departed out of him: and the child was cured from that very hour" (Matthew 17:18).

"And Jesus rebuked him, saying, Hold thy peace, and come out of him. And when the unclean spirit had torn him, and cried with a loud voice, he came out of him. And they were all amazed, insomuch that they questioned among themselves, saying, What thing is this? what new doctrine is this? for with authority commandeth He even the unclean spirits, and they do obey Him. And He healed many that were sick of divers diseases, and cast out many devils; and suffered not the devils to speak, because they knew Him" (Mark 1:25-27,34).

"And unclean spirits, when they saw Him, fell down before Him, and cried, saying, Thou art the Son of God. And He straitly charged them that they should not make Him known" (Mark 3:11,12).

"And He said unto them, this kind can come forth by nothing, but by prayer and fasting" (Mark 9:29).

"And they were all amazed, and spake among themselves, saying, What a word is this! for with authority and power He commandeth the unclean spirits, and they come out. And devils also came out of many, crying out, and saying, Thou art Christ the Son of God. And He rebuking them suffered them not to speak: for they knew that He was Christ" (Luke 4:36,41).

"Behold, I give unto you power to tread on serpents and scorpions, and over all the power of the enemy: and nothing shall by any means hurt you" (Luke 10:19).

"And He was casting out a devil, and it was dumb. And it came to pass, when the devil was gone out, the dumb spake; and the people wondered" (Luke 11:14).

"And He laid his hands on her: and immediately she was made straight, and glorified God. And ought not this woman, being a daughter of Abraham, whom Satan hath bound, lo, these eighteen years, be loosed from this bond on the sabbath day?" (Luke 13:13,16).

"After this manner therefore pray ye: Our Father which art in heaven, Hallowed be Thy name. Thy kingdom come. Thy will be done in earth, as it is in heaven. Give us this day our daily bread. And forgive us our debts, as we forgive our debtors. And lead us not into temptation, but deliver us from evil: For Thine is the kingdom, and the power, and the glory, for ever. Amen. But if ye forgive not men their trespasses, neither will your Father forgive your trespasses."

(Matthew 6:9-13,15)

～ 43 ～

THE PRAYERS OF JESUS

"But I say unto you, Love your enemies, bless them that curse you, do good to them that hate you, and pray for them which despitefully use you, and persecute you" (Matthew 5:44).

"And when thou prayest, thou shalt not be as the hypocrites are: for they love to pray standing in the synagogues and in the corners of the streets, that they may be seen of men. Verily I say unto you, They have their reward. But thou, when thou prayest, enter into thy closet, and when thou hast shut thy door, pray to thy Father which is in secret; and thy Father which seeth in secret shall reward thee openly. But when ye pray, use not vain repetitions, as the heathen do: for they think that they shall be heard for their much speaking. Be not ye therefore like unto them: for your Father knoweth what things ye have need of, before ye ask Him. After this manner therefore pray ye: Our Father which art in heaven, Hallowed be Thy name. Thy kingdom come. Thy will be done in earth, as it is in heaven. Give us this day our daily bread. And forgive us our debts, as we forgive our debtors. And lead us not into temptation, but deliver us from evil: For Thine is the kingdom, and the power, and the glory, for ever. Amen. But if ye forgive not men their trespasses, neither will your Father forgive your trespasses" (Matthew 6:5-13, 15).

"And when He was come into the temple, the chief priests and the elders of the people came unto Him as He was teaching, and said, By what authority doest Thou these things? and who gave Thee this authority?" (Matthew 21:23).

"And in the morning, rising up a great while before day, He went out, and departed into a solitary place, and there prayed" (Mark 1:35).

"But without a parable spake He not unto them: and when they were alone, He expounded all things to His disciples" (Mark 4:34).

"And when He had sent them away, He departed into a mountain to pray" (Mark 6:46).

"And when ye stand praying, forgive, if ye have ought against any: that your Father also which is in heaven may forgive you your trespasses" (Mark 11:25).

"And they came to a place which was named Gethsemane: and He saith to His disciples, Sit ye here, while I shall pray. And He taketh with Him Peter and James and John, and began to be sore amazed, and to be very heavy, And saith unto them, My soul is exceeding sorrowful unto death: tarry ye here, and watch. And He went forward a little, and fell on the ground, and prayed that, if it were possible, the hour might pass from Him. And He said, Abba, Father, all things are possible unto Thee; take away this cup from Me: nevertheless not what I will, but what Thou wilt. And He cometh, and findeth them sleeping, and saith unto Peter, Simon, sleepest thou? couldest not thou watch one hour? Watch ye and pray, lest ye enter into temptation. The spirit truly is ready, but the flesh is weak. And again He went away, and prayed, and spake the same words. And when He returned, He found them alseep again, (for their eyes were heavy,) neither wist they what to answer Him. And He cometh the third time, and saith unto them, Sleep on now, and take your rest: it is enough, the hour is come; behold, the Son of man is betrayed into the hands of sinners. Rise up, let us go; lo, he that betrayeth Me is at hand" (Mark 14:32-42).

"Now when all the people were baptized, it came to pass, that Jesus also being baptized, and praying, the heaven was opened" (Luke 3:21).

"And it came to pass, when He was in a certain city, behold a man full of leprosy: who seeing Jesus fell on his face, and besought Him, saying, Lord, if Thou wilt, Thou canst make me clean. And He withdrew Himself into the wilderness, and prayed" (Luke 5:12,16).

"And it came to pass in those days, that He went out into a mountain to pray, and continued all night in prayer to God" (Luke 6:12).

"Bless them that curse you, and pray for them which despitefully use you" (Luke 6:28).

"And it came to pass, as He was alone praying, His disciples were with Him: and He asked them, saying, Whom say the people that I am? And it came to pass about an eight days after these sayings, he took Peter and John and James, and went up into a mountain to pray. And as He prayed, the fashion of His countenance was altered, and His raiment was white and glistering" (Luke 9:18,28,29).

"And it came to pass, that, as He was praying in a certain place, when He ceased, one of His disciples said unto Him, Lord, teach us to pray, as

John also taught His disciples. And He said unto them, When ye pray, say, Our Father which art in heaven, Hallowed be Thy name. Thy kingdom come. Thy will be done, as in heaven, so in earth. Give us day by day our daily bread. And forgive us our sins; for we also forgive every one that is indebted to us. And lead us not into temptation; but deliver us from evil" (Luke 11:1-4).

"And the Lord said, Simon, Simon, behold, Satan hath desired to have you, that he may sift you as wheat: But I have prayed for thee, that thy faith fail not: and when thou art converted, strengthen thy brethren. And He was withdrawn from them about a stone's cast and kneeled down, and prayed, Saying, Father, if Thou be willing, remove this cup from Me: nevertheless not My will, but Thine, be done. And being in an agony He prayed more earnestly: and His sweat was as it were great drops of blood falling down to the ground. And when He rose up from prayer, and was come to His disciples, He found them sleeping for sorrow" (Luke 22:31,32, 41,42,44,45).

"Who is he that condemneth? It is Christ that died, yea rather, that is risen again, who is even at the right hand of God, who also maketh intercession for us" (Romans 8:34).

"By so much was Jesus made a surety of a better testament. And they truly were many priests, because they were not suffered to continue by reason of death: But this man, because He continueth ever, hath an unchangeable priesthood. Wherefore He is able also to save them to the uttermost that come unto God by Him, seeing He ever liveth to make intercession for them" (Hebrews 7:22-25).

❧ 44 ❧

THE REACTIONS OF JESUS TO CHILDREN

"And Jesus called a little child unto Him, and set Him in the midst of them, And said, Verily I say unto you, Except ye be converted, and become as little children, ye shall not enter into the kingdom of heaven. Whosoever therefore shall humble himself as this little child, the same is greatest in the kingdom of heaven. And whoso shall receive one such little child in My name receiveth Me. But whoso shall offend one of these little ones which believe in Me, it were better for him that a millstone were hanged about his neck, and that he were drowned in the depth of the sea" (Matthew 18:2-6).

"Take heed that ye despise not one of these little ones; for I say unto you, That in heaven their angels do always behold the face of my Father which is in heaven" (Matthew 18:10).

"Then were there brought unto Him little children, that He should put His hands on them, and pray: and the disciples rebuked them. But Jesus said, Suffer little children, and forbid them not, to come unto me: for of such is the kingdom of heaven. And He laid His hands on them, and departed thence" (Matthew 19:13-15).

"And said unto Him, Hearest thou what these

say? And Jesus saith unto them, Yea; have ye never read, Out of the mouth of babes and sucklings thou hast perfected praise?" (Matthew 21:16).

"And He took a child, and set him in the midst of them: and when He had taken him in His arms, He said unto them, Whosoever shall receive one of such children in My name, receiveth Me: and whosoever shall receive Me, receiveth not Me, but Him that sent Me" (Mark 9:36,37).

"And they brought young children to Him, that He should touch them: and His disciples rebuked those that brought them. But when Jesus saw it, He was much displeased, and said unto them, Suffer the little children to come unto Me, and forbid them not: for of such is the kingdom of God. Verily I say unto you, Whosoever shall not receive the kingdom of God as a little child, He shall not enter therein" (Mark 10:13-15).

"If ye then, being evil, know how to give good gifts unto your children: how much more shall your heavenly Father give the Holy Spirit to them that ask Him?" (Luke 11:13).

"O Jerusalem, Jerusalem, which killest the prophets, and stonest them that are sent unto thee; how often would I have gathered thy children together, as a hen doth gather her brood under her wings, and ye would not!" (Luke 13:34).

"And they brought unto Him also infants, that He would touch them: but when His disciples saw it, they rebuked them. But Jesus called them unto Him, and said, Suffer little children to come unto Me, and forbid them not: for of such is the kingdom of God" (Luke 18:15,16).

~ 45 ~

THE REACTIONS OF JESUS TO ENEMIES

"And Jesus knew their thoughts, and said unto them, Every kingdom divided against itself is brought to desolation; and every city or house divided against itself shall not stand: And if Satan cast out Satan, he is divided against himself; how shall then his kingdom stand? But if I cast out devils by the Spirit of God, then the kingdom of God is come unto you. He that is not with Me is against Me; and he that gathereth not with Me scattereth abroad. O generation of vipers, how can ye, being evil, speak good things? for out of the abundance of the heart the mouth speaketh. But He answered and said unto them, An evil and adulterous generation seeketh after a sign; and there shall no sign be given to it, but the sign of the prophet Jonas" (Matthew 12:25, 26,28,30,34,39).

"And they were offended in Him. But Jesus said unto them, A prophet is not without honour, save in His own country, and in His own house" (Matthew 13:57).

"But He answered and said unto them, Why do ye also transgress the commandment of God by your tradition? Ye hypocrites, well did Esaias prophesy of you, saying" (Matthew 15:3,7).

"The Pharisees also with the Sadducees came, and tempting desired Him that He would shew them a sign from heaven. He answered and said unto them, When it is evening, ye say, It will be fair weather: for the sky is red. And in the morning, It will be foul weather to day: for the sky is red and lowering. O ye hypocrites, ye can discern the face of the sky; but can ye not discern the signs of the times? A wicked and adulterous generation seeketh after a sign; and there shall no sign be given unto it, but the sign of the prophet Jonas. And He left them, and departed. But He turned, and said unto Peter, Get thee behind Me, Satan: thou art an offence unto Me: for thou savourest not the things that be of God, but those that be of men" (Matthew 16:1-4,23).

"And immediately when Jesus perceived in His spirit that they so reasoned within themselves, He said unto them, Why reason these things ye in your hearts?" (Mark 2:8).

"But when Jesus perceived their thoughts, He answering said unto them, What reason ye in your hearts? Whether is easier, to say, thy sins be forgiven thee; or to say, Rise up and walk?" (Luke 5:22,23).

"But He, knowing their thoughts, said unto them, Every kingdom divided against itself is brought to desolation; and a house divided against a house falleth. Woe unto you, Pharisees! for ye love the uppermost seats in the synagogues, and greetings in the markets. Woe unto you! for ye build the sepulchres of the prophets, and your fathers killed them. Woe unto you, lawyers! for ye have taken away the key of knowledge: ye entered not in yourselves, and them that were entering in ye hindered" (Luke 11:17,43,47,52).

"The Lord then answered him, and said, Thou hypocrite, doth not each one of you on the sabbath loose his ox or his ass from the stall, and lead him away to watering?" (Luke 13:15).

"And Jesus answering spake unto the lawyers and Pharisees, saying, Is it lawful to heal on the sabbath day? And they held their peace. And He took him, and healed him, and let him go" (Luke 14:3,4).

"And the Pharisees also, who were covetous, heard all these things: and they derided him. And he said unto them, Ye are they which justify yourselves before men; but God knoweth your hearts: for that which is highly esteemed among men is abomination in the sight of God" (Luke 16:14,15).

"Saying, If Thou hadst known, even Thou, at least in this Thy day, the things which belong unto Thy peace! but now they are hid from Thine eyes. And He went into the temple, and began to cast out them that sold therein, and them that bought" (Luke 19:42,45).

"But He perceived their craftiness, and said unto them, Why tempt ye Me?" (Luke 20:23).

"And many other things blasphemously spake they against Him. Art Thou the Christ? tell us. And He said unto them, If I tell you, ye will not believe" (Luke 22:65,67).

"The people answered and said, thou hast a devil: who goeth about to kill thee? Jesus answered and said unto them, I have done one work, and ye all marvel" (John 7:20,21).

"And then shall they see the Son of man coming in the clouds with great power and glory. And then shall He send His angels, and shall gather together His elect from the four winds, from the uttermost part of the earth to the uttermost part of heaven. But of that day and that hour knoweth no man, no, not the angels which are in heaven, neither the Son, but the Father. Watch ye therefore: for ye know not when the master of the house cometh, at even, or at midnight, or at the cockcrowing, or in the morning: And what I say unto you I say unto all, Watch."

(Mark 13:26,27,32,35,37)

≈ 46 ≈

THE RETURN OF JESUS

"For the Son of man shall come in the glory of His Father with His angels; and then He shall reward every man according to his works" (Matthew 16:27).

"And this gospel of the kingdom shall be preached in all the world for a witness unto all nations; and then shall the end come. Then if any man shall say unto you, Lo, here is Christ, or there; believe it not. For as the lightning cometh out of the east, and shineth even unto the west; so shall also the coming of the Son of man be. But as the days of Noe were, so shall also the coming of the Son of man be" (Matthew 24:14,23,27,37).

"And then shall they see the Son of man coming in the clouds with great power and glory. And then shall He send His angels, and shall gather together His elect from the four winds, from the uttermost part of the earth to the uttermost part of heaven. But of that day and that hour knoweth no man, no, not the angels which are in heaven, neither the Son, but the Father. Watch ye therefore: for ye know not when the master of the house cometh, at even, or at midnight, or at the cockcrowing, or in the morning: And what I say unto you I say unto all, Watch" (Mark 13:26,27,32,35,37).

"For as the lightning, that lighteneth out of the one part under heaven, shineth unto the other part under heaven; so shall also the Son of man be in his day. But first must he suffer many things, and be rejected of this generation. And as it was in the days of Noe, so shall it be also in the days of the Son of man. I tell you, in that night there shall be two men in one bed; the one shall be taken, and the other shall be left. Two men shall be in the field; the one shall be taken, and the other left" (Luke 17:24-26, 34,36).

"Verily, verily, I say unto you, The hour is coming, and now is, when the dead shall hear the voice of the Son of God: and they that hear shall live. Marvel not at this: for the hour is coming, in the which all that are in the graves shall hear His voice" (John 5:25,28).

"Which also said, Ye men of Galilee, why stand ye gazing up into heaven? this same Jesus, which is taken up from you into heaven, shall so come in like manner as ye have seen Him go into heaven" (Acts 1:11).

"For as often as ye eat this bread, and drink this cup, ye do shew the Lord's death till He come" (1 Corinthians 11:26).

"Behold, I come quickly: hold that fast which thou hast, that no man take thy crown" (Revelation 3:11).

"For the great day of His wrath is come; and who shall be able to stand?" (Revelation 6:17).

"Behold, I come as a thief. Blessed is he that watcheth, and keepeth his garments, lest he walk naked, and they see his shame" (Revelation 16:15).

"Let us be glad and rejoice, and give honour to Him: for the marriage of the Lamb is come, and His wife hath made herself ready. And I fell at His feet to worship Him. And He said unto me, See thou do it not: I am thy fellowservant, and of thy brethren that have the testimony of Jesus: worship God: for the testimony of Jesus is the spirit of prophecy. And I saw heaven opened, and behold a white horse; and He that sat upon Him was called Faithful and True, and in righteousness He doth judge and make war. His eyes were as a flame of fire, and on His head were many crowns; and He had a name written, that no man knew, but He Himself. And He was clothed with a vesture dipped in blood: and His name is called The Word of God. And the armies which were in heaven followed Him upon white horses, clothed in fine linen, white and clean. And out of His mouth goeth a sharp sword, that with it He should smite the nations: and He shall rule them with a rod of iron: and He treadeth the winepress of the fierceness and wrath of Almighty God. And He hath on His vesture and on His thigh a name written, King Of Kings, And Lord Of Lords" (Revelation 19:7,10-16).

"Whosoever therefore shall humble himself as this little child, the same is greatest in the kingdom of heaven."
                                        (Matthew 18:4)

≈ 47 ≈

THE SECRETS OF SUCCESS OF JESUS

"Leave there thy gift before the altar, and go thy way; first be reconciled to thy brother, and then come and offer thy gift. Give to him that asketh thee, and from him that would borrow of thee turn not thou away" (Matthew 5:24,42).

"Thou hypocrite, first cast out the beam out of thine own eye; and then shalt thou see clearly to cast out the mote out of thy brother's eye. Ask, and it shall be given you; seek, and ye shall find; knock, and it shall be opened unto you" (Matthew 7:5,7).

"And whosoever shall give to drink unto one of these little ones a cup of cold water only in the name of a disciple, verily I say unto you, he shall in no wise lose his reward" (Matthew 10:42).

"For whosoever hath, to him shall be given, and he shall have more abundance: but whosoever hath not, from him shall be taken away even that he hath" (Matthew 13:12).

"And I will give unto thee the keys of the kingdom of heaven: and whatsoever thou shalt bind on earth shall be bound in heaven: and whatsoever thou shalt loose on earth shall be loosed in heaven" (Matthew 16:19).

"Whosoever therefore shall humble himself as

this little child, the same is greatest in the kingdom of heaven" (Matthew 18:4).

"Jesus said unto him, If thou wilt be perfect, go and sell that thou hast, and give to the poor, and thou shalt have treasure in heaven: and come and follow Me" (Matthew 19:21).

"And whosoever shall exalt himself shall be abased; and he that shall humble himself shall be exalted" (Matthew 23:12).

"For unto every one that hath shall be given, and he shall have abundance: but from him that hath not shall be taken away even that which he hath" (Matthew 25:29).

"And He said unto them, Take heed what ye hear: with what measure ye mete, it shall be measured to you: and unto you that hear shall more be given" (Mark 4:24).

"For whosoever shall give you a cup of water to drink in My name, because ye belong to Christ, verily I say unto you, he shall not lose his reward" (Mark 9:41).

"And he said, Abba, Father, all things are possible unto Thee; take away this cup from Me: nevertheless not what I will, but what Thou wilt" (Mark 14:36).

"And as ye would that men should do to you, do ye also to them likewise" (Luke 6:31).

"For every one that asketh receiveth; and he that seeketh findeth; and to him that knocketh it shall be opened" (Luke 11:10).

"Fear not, little flock; for it is your Father's good pleasure to give you the kingdom. Blessed are those servants, whom the lord when he cometh shall find watching: verily I say unto you, that he shall gird himself, and make them to sit down to meat, and will come forth and serve them. And if he shall come in the second watch, or come in the third watch, and find them so, blessed are those servants" (Luke 12:32,37,38).

"And in that day ye shall ask Me nothing. Verily, verily, I say unto you, Whatsoever ye shall ask the Father in My name, He will give it you" (John 16:23).

"Give to him that asketh thee, and from him that would borrow of thee turn not thou away."

(Matthew 5:42)

~ 48 ~

THE TEACHING OF JESUS ON GIVING

"Leave there thy gift before the altar, and go thy way; first be reconciled to thy brother, and then come and offer thy gift" (Matthew 5:24).

"Give to him that asketh thee, and from him that would borrow of thee turn not thou away" (Matthew 5:42).

"Take heed that ye do not your alms before men, to be seen of them: otherwise ye have no reward of your Father which is in heaven. Therefore when thou doest thine alms, do not sound a trumpet before thee, as the hypocrites do in the synagogues and in the streets, that they may have glory of men. Verily I say unto you, they have their reward. But when thou doest alms, let not thy left hand know what thy right hand doeth: That thine alms may be in secret: and thy Father which seeth in secret Himself shall reward thee openly. Lay not up for yourselves treasures upon earth, where moth and rust doth corrupt, and where thieves break through and steal: No man can serve two masters: for either he will hate the one, and love the other; or else he will hold to the one, and despise the other. Ye cannot serve God and mammon. But seek ye first the kingdom of God, and his rightousness; and all these things shall be added unto you. Take therefore no thought for the morrow: for the morrow shall take thought for the things of itself. Sufficient unto the day is the evil thereof" (Matthew 6:1-4,19,24,33,34).

"Ask, and it shall be given you; seek, and ye shall find; knock, and it shall be opened unto you: For every one that asketh receiveth; and he that seeketh findeth; and to him that knocketh it shall be opened. Or what man is there of you, whom if his son ask bread, will he give him a stone? Or if he ask a fish, will he give him a serpent? If ye then, being evil, know how to give good gifts unto your children, how much more shall your Father which is in heaven give good things to them that ask Him?" (Matthew 7:7-11).

"Heal the sick, cleanse the lepers, raise the dead, cast out devils: freely ye have received, freely give" (Matthew 10:8).

"Jesus said unto him, If thou wilt be perfect, go and sell that thou hast, and give to the poor, and thou shalt have treasure in heaven: and come and follow Me" (Matthew 19:21).

"Woe unto you, scribes and Pharisees, hypocrites! for ye pay tithe of mint and anise and cummin, and have omitted the weightier matters of the law, judgement, mercy, and faith: these ought ye to have done, and not to leave the other undone" (Matthew 23:23).

"And He said, so is the kingdom of God, as if a man should cast Seed into the ground; And should sleep, and rise night and day, and the Seed should spring and grow up, he knoweth not how. For the earth bringeth forth fruit of herself; first the blade, then the ear, after that the full corn in the ear. But when the fruit is brought forth, immediately he putteth in the sickle, because the harvest is come" (Mark 4:26).

"For whosoever shall give you a cup of water to drink in My name, because ye belong to Christ, verily I say unto you, he shall not lose his reward" (Mark 9:41).

"Then Jesus beholding him loved him, and said unto him, One thing thou lackest: go thy way, sell whatsoever thou hast, and give to the poor, and thou shalt have treasure in heaven: and come, take up the cross, and follow Me" (Mark 10:21).

"Give, and it shall be given unto you; good measure, pressed down, and shaken together, and running over, shall men give into your bosom. For with the same measure that ye mete withal it shall be measured to you again" (Luke 6:38).

"Sell that ye have, and give alms; provide yourselves bags which wax not old, a treasure in the heavens that faileth not, where no thief approacheth, neither moth corrupteth" (Luke 12:33).

"And if ye have not been faithful in that which is another man's, who shall give you that which is your own?" (Luke 16:12).

"The Pharisees also came unto Him, tempting Him, and saying unto Him, Is it lawful for a man to put away his wife for every cause? And He answered and said unto them, Have ye not read, that He which made them at the beginning made them male and female, And said, For this cause shall a man leave father and mother, and shall cleave to his wife: and they twain shall be one flesh? Wherefore they are no more twain, but one flesh. What therefore God hath joined together, let not man put asunder."   (Matthew 19:3-6)

⇜ 49 ⇝

THE TEACHINGS OF JESUS ON MARRIAGE AND DIVORCE

"It hath been said, Whosoever shall put away his wife, let him give her a writing of divorcement: But I say unto you, That whosoever shall put away his wife, saving for the cause of fornication, causeth her to commit adultery: and whosoever shall marry her that is divorced committeth adultery" (Matthew 5:31,32).

"The Pharisees also came unto Him, tempting Him, and saying unto Him, Is it lawful for a man to put away his wife for every cause? And He answered and said unto them, Have ye not read, that He which made them at the beginning made them male and female, And said, For this cause shall a man leave father and mother, and shall cleave to his wife: and they twain shall be one flesh? Wherefore they are no more twain, but one flesh. What therefore God hath joined together, let not man put asunder. They say unto Him, Why did Moses then command to give a writing of divorcement, and to put her away? He saith unto them, Moses because of the hardness of your hearts suffered you to put away your wives: but from the beginning it was not so. And I say unto you, Whosoever shall put away his wife, except it be for fornication, and shall marry another, committeth adultery: and whoso marrieth her which is put away doth commit adultery. His disciples say unto Him, If the case of the man be so with his wife, it is not good to marry. But He said unto them, All men cannot receive this saying, save they to whom it is given. For there are some eunuchs, which were so born from their mother's womb: and there are some eunuchs, which were made euunchs of men: and there be eunuchs, which have made themselves eunuchs for the kingdom of heaven's sake. He that is able to receive it, let him receive it" (Matthew 19:3-12).

"And the Pharisees came to Him, and asked Him, Is it lawful for a man to put away his wife? tempting Him. And He answered and said unto them, What did Moses command you? And they said, Moses suffered to write a bill of divorcement, and to put her away. And Jesus answered and said unto them, For the hardness of your heart he wrote you this precept. But from the beginning of the creation God made them male and female. For this cause shall a man leave his father and mother, and cleave to his wife; And they twain shall be one flesh: so then they are no more twain, but one flesh. What therefore God hath joined together, let not man put asunder. And in the house His disciples asked Him again of the same matter. And He saith unto them, Whosoever shall put away his wife, and marry another, committeth adultery against her. And if a woman shall put away her husband, and be married to another, she committeth adultery" (Mark 10:2-12).

"For when they shall rise from the dead, they neither marry, nor are given in marriage; but are as the angels which are in heaven" (Mark 12:25).

"Whosoever putteth away his wife, and marrieth another, committeth adultery: and whosoever marrieth her that is put away from her husband committeth adultery" (Luke 16:18).

"And Jesus answering said unto them, The children of this world marry, and are given in marriage: But they which shall be accounted worthy to obtain that world, and the resurrection from the dead, neither marry, nor are given in marriage" (Luke 20:34,35).

"And when He was come near, He beheld the city, and wept over it."
(Luke 19:41)

≈ 50 ≈

THE TEARS OF JESUS

"He is despised and rejected of men; a man of sorrows, and acquainted with grief: and we hid as it were our faces from Him; He was despised, and we esteemed Him not. Surely He hath borne our griefs, and carried our sorrows: yet we did esteem Him stricken, smitten of God, and afflicted. But He was wounded for our transgressions, He was bruised for our iniquities: the chastisement of our peace was upon Him; and with His stripes we are healed" (Isaiah 53:3-5).

"And about the ninth hour Jesus cried with a loud voice, saying, Eli, Eli, lama sabachthani? that is to say, My God, My God, why hast Thou forsaken Me? Some of them that stood there, when they heard that, said, This man calleth for Elias" (Matthew 27:46,47).

"And when He was come near, He beheld the city, and wept over it" (Luke 19:41).

"And being in an agony He prayed more earnestly: and His sweat was as it were great drops of blood falling down to the ground" (Luke 22:44).

"When Jesus therefore saw her weeping, and the Jews also weeping which came with her, He groaned in the spirit, and was troubled, And said, Where have ye laid him? They said unto Him, Lord, come and see. Jesus wept" (John 11:33-35).

"Now is My soul troubled; and what shall I say? Father, save Me from this hour: but for this cause came I unto this hour" (John 12:27).

∽ 51 ∽

THE TEMPTATIONS OF JESUS

———➤●←———

"Then was Jesus led up of the Spirit into the wilderness to be tempted of the devil. And when He had fasted forty days and forty nights, He was afterward an hungred. And when the tempter came to Him, he said, If thou be the Son of God, command that these stones be made bread. But He answered and said, It is written, Man shall not live by bread alone, but by every word that proceedeth out of the mouth of God. Jesus said unto him, It is written again, Thou shalt not tempt the Lord thy God. Then saith Jesus unto him, Get thee hence, Satan: for it is written, Thou shalt worship the Lord thy God, and Him only shalt thou serve" (Matthew 4:1-4,7,10).

"The Pharisees also with the Sadducees came, and tempting desired Him that He would shew them a sign from heaven. He answered and said unto them, When it is evening, ye say, It will be fair weather: for the sky is red. And in the morning, It will be foul weather to day: for the sky is red and lowering. O ye hypocrites, ye can discern the face of the sky; but can ye not discern the signs of the times?" (Matthew 16:1-3).

"But Jesus perceived their wickedness, and said, Why tempt ye Me, ye hypocrites? Then one of them, which was a lawyer, asked Him a question, tempting Him, and saying, Master, which is the great commandment in the law? Jesus said unto him, Thou shalt love the Lord thy God with all thy heart, and with all thy soul, and with all thy mind. This is the first and great commandment. And the second is like unto it, Thou shalt love thy neighbor as thyself. On these two commandments hang all the law and the prophets" (Matthew 22:18,35-40).

"And He was there in the wilderness forty days, tempted of Satan; and was with the wild beasts; and the angels ministered unto Him" (Mark 1:13).

"And the Pharisees came forth, and began to question with Him, seeking of Him a sign from heaven, tempting Him" (Mark 8:11).

"And the Pharisees came to Him, and asked Him, Is it lawful for a man to put away his wife? tempting Him. And He answered and said unto them, What did Moses command you? And they said, Moses suffered to write a bill of divorcement, and to put her away. And Jesus answered and said unto them, For the hardness of your heart he wrote you this precept" (Mark 10:2-5).

"Shall we give, or shall we not give? But He, knowing their hypocrisy, said unto them, Why tempt ye Me? bring Me a penny, that I may see it" (Mark 12:15).

"Watch ye and pray, lest ye enter into temptation. The spirit truly is ready, but the flesh is weak" (Mark 14:38).

"And Jesus being full of the Holy Ghost returned from Jordan, and was led by the Spirit into the wilderness, Being forty days tempted of the devil.

And in those days He did eat nothing: and when they were ended, He afterward hungered. And Jesus answering said unto him, It is said, Thou shalt not tempt the Lord thy God. And when the devil had ended all the temptation, he departed from Him for a season" (Luke 4:1-2,12,13).

"And, behold, a certain lawyer stood up, and tempted Him, saying, Master, what shall I do to inherit eternal life?" (Luke 10:25).

"But He perceived their craftiness, and said unto them, Why tempt ye Me? Shew Me a penny. Whose image and superscription hath it? They answered and said, Caesar's. And He said unto them, Render therefore unto Caesar the things which be Caesar's, and unto God the things which be God's" (Luke 20:23-25).

"This they said, tempting Him, that they might have to accuse Him. But Jesus stooped down, and with His finger wrote on the ground, as though He heard them not. So when they continued asking Him, He lifted up Himself, and said unto them, He that is without sin among you, let him first cast a stone at her. And again He stooped down, and wrote on the ground. And they which heard it, being convicted by their own conscience, went out one by one, beginning at the eldest, even unto the last: and Jesus was left alone, and the woman standing in the midst. When Jesus had lifted up Himself, and saw none but the woman, He said unto her, Woman, where are those thine accusers? hath no man condemned thee? She said, No man, Lord. And Jesus said unto her, Neither do I condemn thee: go, and sin no more" (John 8:6-11).

"There hath no temptation taken you but such as is common to man: but God is faithful, who will not suffer you to be tempted above that ye are able; but will with the temptation also make a way to escape, that ye may be able to bear it" (1 Corinthians 10:13).

"For in that He Himself hath suffered being tempted, He is able to succour them that are tempted" (Hebrews 2:18).

"For we have not an high priest which cannot be touched with the feeling of our infirmities; but was in all points tempted like as we are, yet without sin. Let us therefore come boldly unto the throne of grace, that we may obtain mercy, and find grace to help in time of need" (Hebrews 4:15,16).

≈ 52 ≈

THE TRIUMPH OF JESUS

"He will swallow up death in victory; and the Lord God will wipe away tears from off all faces; and the rebuke of His people shall He take away from off all the earth: for the Lord hath spoken it" (Isaiah 25:8).

"Then saith He to the disciple, Behold thy mother! And from that hour that disciple took her unto his own home. After this, Jesus knowing that all things were now accomplished, that the scripture might be fulfilled, saith, I thirst. When Jesus therefore had received the vinegar, He said, It is finished: and He bowed His head, and gave up the ghost" (John 19:27,28,30).

"O death, where is thy sting? O grave, where is thy victory? The sting of death is sin; and the strength of sin is the law. But thanks be to God, which giveth us the victory through our Lord Jesus Christ" (1 Corinthians 15:55-57).

"Now thanks be unto God, which always causeth us to triumph in Christ, and maketh manifest the savour of His knowledge by us in every place" (2 Corinthians 2:14).

"And having spoiled principalities and powers, He made a shew of them openly, triumphing over them in it" (Colossians 2:15).

"But is now made manifest by the appearing of

our Saviour Jesus Christ, who hath abolished death, and hath brought life and immortality to light through the gospel" (2 Timothy 1:10).

"But we see Jesus, who was made a little lower than the angels for the suffering of death, crowned with glory and honour; that He by the grace of God should taste death for every man. For it became Him, for Whom are all things, and by Whom are all things, in bringing many sons unto glory, to make the captain of their salvation perfect through sufferings" (Hebrews 2:9,10).

"For Christ also hath once suffered for sins, the just for the unjust, that He might bring us to God, being put to death in the flesh, but quickened by the Spirit" (1 Peter 3:18).

"He that committeth sin is of the devil; for the devil sinneth from the beginning. For this purpose the son of God was manifested, that He might destroy the works of the devil" (1 John 3:8).

"I am He that liveth, and was dead; and, behold, I am alive for evermore, Amen; and have the keys of hell and of death" (Revelation 1:18).

"These shall make war with the Lamb, and the Lamb shall overcome them: for He is Lord of lords, and King of kings: and they that are with Him are called, and chosen, and faithful" (Revelation 17:14).

"Blessed and holy is he that hath part in the first resurrection: on such the second death hath no power, but they shall be priests of God and of Christ, and shall reign with him a thousand years" (Revelation 20:6).

Clip and Mail

251

ORDER FORM THE MIKE MURDOCK WISDOM LIBRARY
(All books paperback unless indicated otherwise.)

QTY	CODE	BOOK TITLE	USA	TOTAL
	B01	WISDOM FOR WINNING	$10	
	B02	5 STEPS OUT OF DEPRESSION	$ 3	
	B03	THE SEX TRAP	$ 3	
	B04	10 LIES PEOPLE BELIEVE ABOUT MONEY	$ 3	
	B05	FINDING YOUR PURPOSE IN LIFE	$ 3	
	B06	CREATING TOMORROW THROUGH SEED-FAITH	$ 3	
	B07	BATTLE TECHNIQUES FOR WAR WEARY SAINTS	$ 3	
	B08	ENJOYING THE WINNING LIFE	$ 3	
	B09	FOUR FORCES/GUARANTEE CAREER SUCCESS	$ 3	
	B10	THE BRIDGE CALLED DIVORCE	$ 3	
	B11	DREAM SEEDS	$ 9	
	B12	YOUNG MINISTERS HANDBOOK	$20	
	B13	SEEDS OF WISDOM ON DREAMS AND GOALS	$ 3	
	B14	SEEDS OF WISDOM ON RELATIONSHIPS	$ 3	
	B15	SEEDS OF WISDOM ON MIRACLES	$ 3	
	B16	SEEDS OF WISDOM ON SEED-FAITH	$ 3	
	B17	SEEDS OF WISDOM ON OVERCOMING	$ 3	
	B18	SEEDS OF WISDOM ON HABITS	$ 3	
	B19	SEEDS OF WISDOM ON WARFARE	$ 3	
	B20	SEEDS OF WISDOM ON OBEDIENCE	$ 3	
	B21	SEEDS OF WISDOM ON ADVERSITY	$ 3	
	B22	SEEDS OF WISDOM ON PROSPERITY	$ 3	
	B23	SEEDS OF WISDOM ON PRAYER	$ 3	
	B24	SEEDS OF WISDOM ON FAITH-TALK	$ 3	
	B25	SEEDS OF WISDOM ONE YEAR DEVOTIONAL	$10	
	B26	THE GOD BOOK	$10	
	B27	THE JESUS BOOK	$10	
	B28	THE BLESSING BIBLE	$10	
	B29	THE SURVIVAL BIBLE	$10	
	B30	THE TEEN'S TOPICAL BIBLE	$ 6	
	B30L	THE TEEN'S TOPICAL BIBLE (LEATHER)	$20	
	B31	THE ONE-MINUTE TOPICAL BIBLE	$10	
	B32	THE MINISTER'S TOPICAL BIBLE	$ 6	
	B33	THE BUSINESSMAN'S TOPICAL BIBLE	$ 6	
	B33L	THE BUSINESSMAN'S TOPICAL BIBLE (LEATHER)	$20	
	B34L	THE GRANDPARENT'S TOPICAL BIBLE (LEATHER)	$20	
	B35	THE FATHER'S TOPICAL BIBLE	$ 6	
	B35L	THE FATHER'S TOPICAL BIBLE (LEATHER)	$20	
	B36	THE MOTHER'S TOPICAL BIBLE	$ 6	
	B36L	THE MOTHER'S TOPICAL BIBLE (LEATHER)	$20	
	B37	THE NEW CONVERT'S TOPICAL BIBLE	$15	
	B38	THE WIDOW'S TOPICAL BIBLE	$ 6	
	B39	THE DOUBLE DIAMOND PRINCIPLE	$ 9	
	B40	WISDOM FOR CRISIS TIMES	$ 9	
	B41	THE GIFT OF WISDOM (VOLUME ONE)	$ 8	
	B42	ONE-MINUTE BUSINESSMAN'S DEVOTIONAL	$10	
	B43	ONE-MINUTE BUSINESSWOMAN'S DEVOTIONAL	$10	
	B44	31 SECRETS FOR CAREER SUCCESS	$10	
	B45	101 WISDOM KEYS	$ 7	
	B46	31 FACTS ABOUT WISDOM	$ 7	
	B47	THE COVENANT OF THE FIFTY-EIGHT BLESSINGS	$ 8	
	B48	31 KEYS TO A NEW BEGINNING	$ 7	
	B49	THE PROVERBS 31 WOMAN	$ 7	
	B50	ONE-MINUTE POCKET BIBLE FOR THE ACHIEVER	$ 5	
	B51	ONE-MINUTE POCKET BIBLE FOR FATHERS	$ 5	
	B52	ONE-MINUTE POCKET BIBLE FOR MOTHERS	$ 5	

Qty	Code	Book Title	USA	Total
	B53	One-Minute Pocket Bible For Teenagers	$ 5	
	B54	One-Minute Devotional (hardback)	$14	
	B55	20 Keys To A Happier Marriage	$ 3	
	B56	How To Turn Mistakes Into Miracles	$ 3	
	B57	31 Secrets Of The Unforgettable Woman	$ 9	
	B58	Mentor's Manna On Attitude	$ 3	
	B59	The Making Of A Champion	$ 6	
	B60	One-Minute Pocket Bible For Men	$ 5	
	B61	One-Minute Pocket Bible For Women	$ 5	
	B62	One-Minute Pocket Bible/Bus.Professionals	$ 5	
	B63	One-Minute Pocket Bible For Truckers	$ 5	
	B64	7 Obstacles To Abundant Success	$ 3	
	B65	Born To Taste The Grapes	$ 3	
	B66	Greed, Gold And Giving	$ 3	
	B67	Gift Of Wisdom For Champions	$ 8	
	B68	Gift Of Wisdom For Achievers	$ 8	
	B69	Wisdom Keys For A Powerful Prayer Life	$ 3	
	B70	Gift Of Wisdom For Mothers	$ 8	
	B71	Wisdom - God's Golden Key To Success	$ 7	
	B72	The Greatest Success Habit On Earth	$ 3	
	B73	The Mentor's Manna On Abilities	$ 3	
	B74	The Assignment: Dream/Destiny #1	$10	
	B75	The Assignment: Anointing/Adversity #2	$10	
	B76	The Mentor's Manna On The Assignment	$ 3	
	B77	The Gift Of Wisdom For Fathers	$ 8	
	B78	The Mentor's Manna On The Secret Place	$ 3	
	B79	The Mentor's Manna On Achievement	$ 3	
	B80	The Double Diamond Daily Devotional	$12	
	B81	The Mentor's Manna On Adversity	$ 3	
	B82	31 Reasons People Do Not Receive Their Financial Harvest	$12	
	B83	The Gift Of Wisdom For Wives	$ 8	
	B84	The Gift Of Wisdom For Husbands	$ 8	
	B85	The Gift Of Wisdom For Teenagers	$ 8	
	B86	The Gift Of Wisdom For Leaders	$ 8	
	B87	The Gift Of Wisdom For Graduates	$ 8	
	B88	The Gift Of Wisdom For Brides	$ 8	
	B89	The Gift Of Wisdom For Grooms	$ 8	
	B90	The Gift Of Wisdom For Ministers	$ 8	
	B91H	The Leadership Secrets Of Jesus (hdbk)	$15	
	B92	Secrets Of The Journey (Vol. 1)	$ 5	
	B93	Secrets Of The Journey (Vol. 2)	$ 5	
	B94	Secrets Of The Journey (Vol. 3)	$ 5	
	B95	Secrets Of The Journey (Vol. 4)	$ 5	

❏ CASH   ❏ CHECK   ❏ MONEY ORDER

❏ CREDIT CARD #   ❏ VISA   ❏ MC   ❏ AMEX

EXPIRATION DATE ☐☐☐☐   *SORRY NO C.O.D.'s*

Signature _____

TOTAL PAGE 2	$
TOTAL PAGE 1	$
*ADD SHIPPING 10% USA/20% OTHERS	$
CANADA CURRENCY DIFFERENCE ADD 20%	$
TOTAL ENCLOSED	$

PLEASE PRINT

Name ☐☐☐☐☐☐☐☐☐☐☐☐☐☐☐☐☐☐☐

Address ☐☐☐☐☐☐☐☐☐☐☐☐☐☐☐☐☐☐☐
                              State   Zip
City ☐☐☐☐☐☐☐☐☐☐☐☐☐☐☐☐☐☐☐

Phone (☐☐☐) ☐☐☐-☐☐☐☐

MIKE MURDOCK

- Began full-time evangelism at the age of 19, which has continued for 34 years.

- Has traveled and spoken to more than 14,000 audiences in 36 countries, including East Africa, the Orient, and Europe.

- Noted author of 115 books, including best sellers, *Wisdom for Winning, Dream Seeds and The Double Diamond Principle.*

- Created the popular *"Wisdom Topical Bible"* series for Businessmen, Mothers, Fathers, Teenagers, and the *One-Minute Pocket Bible.*

- Has composed more than 5,600 songs such as *I Am Blessed, You Can Make It, and Jesus Just The Mention Of Your Name,* recorded by many artists.

- Is the Founder of the Wisdom Center in Dallas, Texas.

- Has a weekly television program called *"Wisdom Keys With Mike Murdock".*

- He has appeared often on TBN, CBN, Oral Roberts and other television network programs.

- Is a Founding Trustee on the Board of International Charismatic Bible Ministries founded by Oral Roberts.

- Has seen over 3,400 accept the call into full-time ministry under his ministry.

- Has embraced his Assignment: *Pursuing... Possessing... And Publishing The Wisdom Of God To Heal The Broken In This Generation.*

252

THE MINISTRY

1 **Wisdom Books & Literature** -115 best-selling Wisdom books and Teaching tapes that teach the Wisdom of God to thousands.

2 **Church Crusades** - Multitudes are ministered to in crusades and seminars throughout America in "The Uncommon Wisdom Conferences."

3 **Music Ministry** - Millions have been blessed by the anointed songwriting and singing of Mike Murdock, who has written over 5,600 songs.

4 **Television** - "Wisdom Keys With Mike Murdock," a nationally-syndicated weekly television program.

5 **The Wisdom Center** - Where Dr. Murdock holds annual Schools of Ministry for those training for a more excellent ministry.

6 **Schools of the Holy Spirit** - Mike Murdock hosts Schools of the Holy Spirit to mentor believers on the Person and companionship of the Holy Spirit.

7 **Schools of Wisdom** - Each year Mike Murdock hosts Schools of Wisdom for those who want personalized and advanced training for achieving "The Uncommon Dream."

8 **Missionary Ministry** - Dr. Murdock's overseas outreaches to 36 countries have included crusades to East Africa, South America, and Europe.

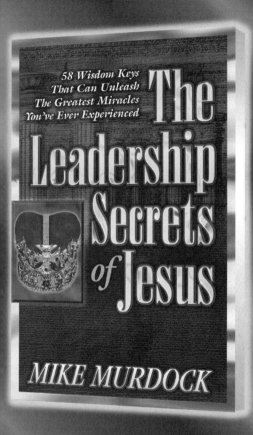

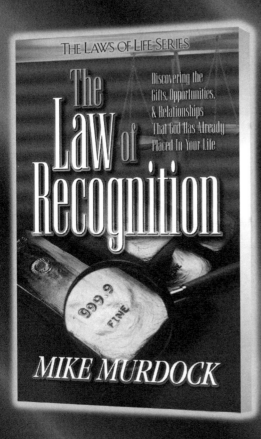

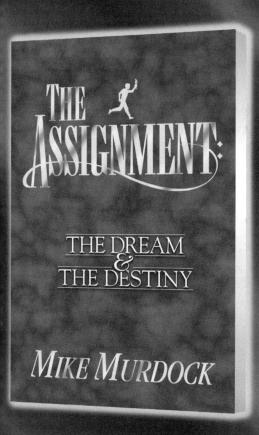

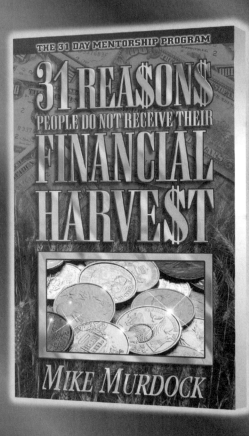

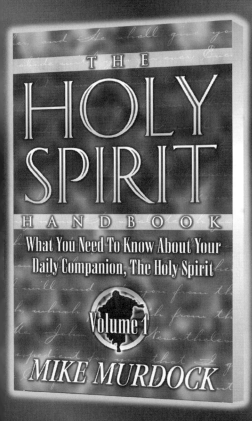

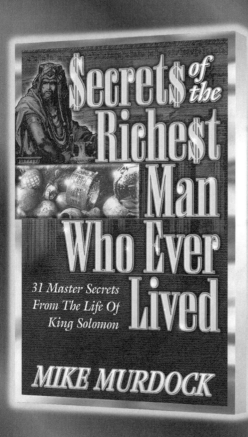